THE PILLOWMAN

BY MARTIN McDONAGH

★

★

DRAMATISTS
PLAY SERVICE
INC.

THE PILLOWMAN
Copyright © 2003, Martin McDonagh

All Rights Reserved

SPECIAL NOTE

THE PILLOWMAN was first presented by the National Theatre at the Cottesloe, London, directed by John Crowley, on November 13, 2003.

The production was subsequently produced on Broadway by the National Theatre, Robert Boyett Theatricals LLC and RMJF Inc. in association with Boyett Ostar, Robert Fox, Arielle Tepper, Stephanie P. McClelland, Debra Black, Dede Harris / Morton Swinsky / Roy Furman / Jon Avnet in association with Joyce Schweickert, opening at the Booth Theatre, New York City, on April 10, 2005.

THE PILLOWMAN was originally produced by the National Theatre at the Cottesloe in London, England, opening on November 13, 2003. It was directed by John Crowley; the set and costume design were by Scott Pask; the lighting design was by Hugh Vanstone; the sound design was by Paul Arditti; and the original music was by Paddy Cunneen. The cast was as follows:

TUPOLSKI	Jim Broadbent
KATURIAN	David Tennant
ARIEL	Nigel Lindsay
MICHAL	Adam Godley
MOTHER	Victoria Pembroke
FATHER	Mike Sherman

THE PILLOWMAN was originally produced in the United States on Broadway at the Booth Theatre in New York City, opening on April 10, 2005. It was produced by the National Theatre, Robert Boyett Theatricals LLC and RMJF Inc. in association with Boyett Ostar, Robert Fox, Arielle Tepper, Stephanie P. McClelland, Debra Black, Dede Harris / Morton Swinsky / Roy Furman / Jon Avnet in association with Joyce Schweickert. It was directed by John Crowley; the set and costume design were by Scott Pask; the lighting design was by Brian MacDevitt; the sound design was by Paul Arditti; and the original music was by Paddy Cunneen. The cast was as follows:

TUPOLSKI	Jeff Goldblum
KATURIAN	Billy Crudup
ARIEL	Željko Ivanek
MICHAL	Michael Stuhlbarg
MOTHER	Virginia Louise Smith
FATHER	Ted Kōch
BOY	Jesse Shane Bronstein
GIRL	Madeleine Martin
MAN	Rick Holmes

CHARACTERS

TUPOLSKI

KATURIAN

ARIEL

MICHAL

MOTHER

FATHER

BOY

GIRL

THE PILLOWMAN

ACT ONE

Scene 1

Police interrogation room. Katurian sitting at table, centre, blindfolded. Tupolski and Ariel enter and sit opposite him, Tupolski with a box file containing a large sheaf of papers.

TUPOLSKI. Mister Katurian, this is Detective Ariel, I'm Detective Tupolski ... Who left that on you?
KATURIAN. What? *(Tupolski takes the blindfold off.)*
TUPOLSKI. Who left this on you?
KATURIAN. Um, the man.
TUPOLSKI. Why didn't you take it off? It just looks stupid.
KATURIAN. I didn't think I was supposed to.
TUPOLSKI. It just looks stupid.
KATURIAN. *(Pause.)* Yes.
TUPOLSKI. *(Pause.)* Like I was saying, this is Detective Ariel and I'm Detective Tupolski.
KATURIAN. Well, the main thing I want to say is, I have complete respect for you and for what you do and I'm glad to help you in any way I can. I have complete respect.
TUPOLSKI. Well, that's good to hear.
KATURIAN. I'm not like some of these ... you know?
TUPOLSKI. Some of these what? I *don't* know?
KATURIAN. Some of these types of people who have no respect for the police. I have never been in trouble with the police in my life. In my life. And I ...
ARIEL. Never been in trouble until now, you mean.
KATURIAN. Hah?

5

ARIEL. Repeating myself ... You have never been in trouble with the police until now. You mean.

KATURIAN. I'm in trouble with the police now?

ARIEL. What else are you doing here?

KATURIAN. I'm helping you with your enquiries, I thought.

ARIEL. So we're friends of yours, like we've took you here like this is a social visit like we're friends of yours?

KATURIAN. You're not friends of mine, no ...

ARIEL. You have had your rights read. You've been took out of your home. You've had a fucking blindfold on. Do you think we do this to our good fucking friends?

KATURIAN. We're not friends, no. But by the same token, I hope we're not enemies.

ARIEL. *(Pause.)* I am going to hit you so hard in the fucking head.

KATURIAN. *(Pause.)* Hah?

ARIEL. Am I mumbling? Tupolski, am I mumbling?

TUPOLSKI. No, you're not mumbling. You're quite clear.

ARIEL. I didn't think I was mumbling.

KATURIAN. You don't ... I will answer everything you want me to. You don't have to ...

ARIEL. "You will answer everything we want you to." There was never a question, "You will answer everything we want you to." There *was* a question, "How much are you going to make us fuck you up in the meantime?" was what the question was.

KATURIAN. I am going to try not to make you fuck me up at all because the reason is I will answer everything.

TUPOLSKI. Well, that's a start, isn't it? *(Eyeing Katurian, Ariel idles to a side wall, smokes a cigarette.)* Why do you suspect we have brought you here? You must suspect some reason.

ARIEL. Look, why don't we just start torturing him and cut out all this shit?

KATURIAN. What...?

TUPOLSKI. Who's the Number One on this case, Ariel, me or you? *(Pause.)* Thank you. Don't listen to him. Anyway, so why do you suspect we have brought you here?

KATURIAN. I've been racking my brains, but I can't think.

TUPOLSKI. You've been racking your brains but you can't think?

KATURIAN. No.

TUPOLSKI. Well, yes or no?

KATURIAN. Yes.

TUPOLSKI. Huh?

KATURIAN. Because I've never done anything. I've never done any anti-police thing, I've never done any anti-state thing ...

TUPOLSKI. You've been racking your brains but you can't think of a single reason we might have brought you here?

KATURIAN. I can think of a reason, or, not a reason but a thing I assume there must be a linkage, although I can't see how there can be a linkage.

TUPOLSKI. The linkage of what? Of what to what? Or, of what to what?

KATURIAN. What? Just, only the thing of how you took my stories away too when you took me, and that you have them there, is the only thing.

TUPOLSKI. And that I have them where? Have you been reading the papers I've got in front of me?

KATURIAN. I haven't been reading ...

TUPOLSKI. Papers which, for all you know, may have been some immensely classified, very very secret thing.

KATURIAN. My eyes caught the titles, just glancing.

TUPOLSKI. Oh, like your peripheral vision?

KATURIAN. Yes.

TUPOLSKI. But, hang on, for it to be your peripheral vision, you'd have to be turned around this way ... (*Tupolski turns sideways on, glancing down at papers.*) See, like this way. Like sideways, like this way ...

KATURIAN. I meant ...

TUPOLSKI. See? Like this way. Like sideways.

KATURIAN. I meant my peripheral vision at the bottom of my eyes.

TUPOLSKI. Ohh, the peripheral vision at the *bottom* of your eyes.

KATURIAN. I don't know if there's a word for that.

TUPOLSKI. There isn't. (*Pause.*) Why would there be a linkage, your stories, you being taken here? It isn't a crime, you write a story.

KATURIAN. That's what I thought.

TUPOLSKI. Given certain restrictions ...

KATURIAN. Of course.

TUPOLSKI. The security of the state, the security of the general whatever-you-call-it. I wouldn't even call them restrictions.

KATURIAN. *I* wouldn't call them restrictions.

TUPOLSKI. I would call them guidelines.

KATURIAN. Guidelines, yes.

TUPOLSKI. Given certain guidelines, the security of the whatever, it isn't a crime, you write a story.

KATURIAN. That's what I thought. That's the whole thing.

TUPOLSKI. What's the whole thing?

KATURIAN. I mean, I agree. You read these things, these "stories," supposedly, "The police are all this," "The government is all this." All these political ... what would you call 'em? "The government should be doing this." Please. Fuck off. You know what I say? I say if you've got a political axe to grind, if you've got a political what-do-ya-call-it, go write a fucking essay, I will know where I stand. I say keep your left-wing this, keep your right-wing that and tell me a fucking story! You know? A great man once said, "The first duty of a storyteller is to tell a story," and I believe in that wholeheartedly, "The first duty of a storyteller is to tell a story." Or was it "The *only* duty of a storyteller is to tell a story"? Yeah, it might have been "The *only* duty of a storyteller is to tell a story." I can't remember, but anyway, that's what I do, I tell stories. No axe to grind, no anything to grind. No social anything whatsoever. And that's why, I can't see, if that's why you've brought me in here, I can't see what the reason would be, unless something political came in by accident, or something that *seemed* political came in, in which case show me where it is. Show me where the bastard is. I'll take it straight out. Fucking burn it. You know? *(Pause. Tupolski stares straight at him.)* You know what I mean?

TUPOLSKI. I have to fill this form out now. It's a form in case anything bad happens to you in custody. *(Pause.)* We've got a mistake here with your name, I think. Your surname is Katurian, yes?

KATURIAN. Yes.

TUPOLSKI. See, we've got your first name as Katurian.

KATURIAN. My first name *is* Katurian.

TUPOLSKI. *(Pause.)* Your first name is Katurian?

KATURIAN. Yes.

TUPOLSKI. And your second name is Katurian?

KATURIAN. Yes.

TUPOLSKI. Your name is Katurian Katurian?

KATURIAN. My parents were funny people.

TUPOLSKI. Hm. Middle initial?

KATURIAN. K. *(Tupolski looks at him. Katurian nods, shrugs.)*

TUPOLSKI. Your name is Katurian Katurian Katurian?

KATURIAN. Like I said, my parents were funny people.

TUPOLSKI. Mm. For "funny" I guess read "stupid fucking idiots."

KATURIAN. I'm not disagreeing.

TUPOLSKI. Your address is Kamenice 4443?

KATURIAN. Yes.

TUPOLSKI. Which you share with…?

KATURIAN. My brother. Michal.

TUPOLSKI. Ah, Michal. At least it's not fucking "Katurian"!

ARIEL. He's backward, your brother, yeah?

KATURIAN. He's not backward, no. He's slow to get things sometimes.

ARIEL. He's slow to get things. Okay.

TUPOLSKI. Next of kin?

KATURIAN. Michal. My next of kin?

TUPOLSKI. Just formalities, Katurian. You know what I mean? *(Pause.)* Place of work.

KATURIAN. The Kamenice abattoir.

ARIEL. This writer.

KATURIAN. It's not so bad.

TUPOLSKI. You like your work there?

KATURIAN. No, but it's not so bad.

ARIEL. Cutting up animals.

KATURIAN. I don't cut stuff. I just clear stuff.

ARIEL. Oh, you don't cut stuff. You just clear stuff.

KATURIAN. Yes.

ARIEL. I see.

KATURIAN. I just clear it.

ARIEL. You just clear it. You don't cut it.

KATURIAN. Yes.

ARIEL. I see. *(Pause. Tupolski puts his pen down, then tears the form he has been filling in in two.)*

TUPOLSKI. That *wasn't* a form in case anything bad happens to you in custody. I was just mucking around.

KATURIAN. What was it?

TUPOLSKI. It was a piece of paper I was about to tear in two. *(Tupolski flips through the sheaf of stories till he finds the one he is looking for.)* Here we are, "The Little Apple Men."

KATURIAN. What about it? *(Ariel idles back to table, sits, stubs cigarette out, as Tupolski familiarises himself with the story.)* It's not one of my best. *(Pause.)* It's pretty good, though.

TUPOLSKI. This is a story, it starts off, there is a little girl, and her father treats her badly …

KATURIAN. He slaps her around and that. He's a …

TUPOLSKI. You seem to have a lot of st … He's a what?

KATURIAN. What?

9

TUPOLSKI. The father.

ARIEL. "He's a ... " something, you said.

TUPOLSKI. He represents something, does he?

KATURIAN. He represents a bad father. He *is* a bad father. How do you mean, "represents"?

TUPOLSKI. He is a bad father.

KATURIAN. Yes. He slaps the little girl around.

TUPOLSKI. This is why he is a bad father.

KATURIAN. Yes.

TUPOLSKI. What else does he do to the little girl, "he is a bad father"?

KATURIAN. All the story says, I think, is the father treats the little girl badly. You can draw your own conclusions.

ARIEL. Oh, we can draw our own conclusions, now, can we?

KATURIAN. Hah?

ARIEL. You're telling us we can draw our own conclusions now, are you?!

KATURIAN. No! Yes!

ARIEL. We *know* we can draw our own fucking conclusions!

KATURIAN. I know.

ARIEL. Hah?

KATURIAN. I know.

ARIEL. Fucking ... hah?! *(Ariel gets up and paces.)*

TUPOLSKI. Ariel's getting a bit aggrieved because "We can draw our own conclusions" is, sort of, *our job. (Pause.)* And the first conclusion we are drawing is exactly how many stories have you got "a little girl is treated badly," or "a little boy is treated badly"?

KATURIAN. A few. A few.

ARIEL. "A few." I'll say a fucking few. The first fucking twenty we picked up was "a little girl is fucked over in this way, or a little boy is fucked over in this way"...!

KATURIAN. But that isn't saying anything, I'm not trying to say anything ...

ARIEL. You're not what?

KATURIAN. What?

ARIEL. Not what?

KATURIAN. What, are you trying to say that I'm trying to say that the children represent something?

ARIEL. "I am trying to say"...?

KATURIAN. That the children represent The People, or something?

ARIEL. *(Approaching.)* "I am trying to say." He's putting words

10

into my fucking mouth now, "I am trying to say," let alone draw our own fucking conclusions …

KATURIAN. No…!

ARIEL. We can't even speak now, this fucking man says! Put your fucking hands down…! *(Ariel pulls Katurian off his chair by the hair, kneels across him and gouges into his face. Tupolski looks at this, sighs.)*

TUPOLSKI. Any time you're ready, Ariel? *(Ariel stops, breathing heavily, goes back to his seat. To Katurian:)* Retake your seat, please. *(In pain, Katurian does so.)* Oh, I almost forgot to mention … I'm the good cop, he's the bad cop. *(Pause.)* So, back to literature. The father, as we have established, treats the little girl badly, and one day the girl gets some apples and carves some little men out of these apples, all little fingers, little eyes, little toes, and she gives them to her father but she says to him they're *not* to be eaten, they're to be kept as a memento of when his only little daughter was young, and naturally the pig of a father swallows a bunch of these applemen whole, just to spite her, and they have razor blades in them, and he dies in agony.

KATURIAN. And that's kind of like the end of the story, that should be like the end of the story, the father gets his come-uppance. But then it goes on.

TUPOLSKI. But then it goes on. The girl wakes up that night. A number of applemen are walking up her chest. They hold her mouth open. They say to her …

KATURIAN. *(Slight voice.)* "You killed our little brothers … "

TUPOLSKI. "You killed our little brothers." They climb down her throat. She chokes to death on her own blood. The end.

KATURIAN. It's a bit of a twist. You think it's a dream sequence. It isn't. *(Pause.)* What? I said it wasn't my best one.

ARIEL. You hang out round the Jew quarter, Katurian?

KATURIAN. The Jew quarter? No. Now and then I pass through there. I collect my brother the Lamenec district, his school. It's not the Jewish quarter. You go through the Jewish quarter.

ARIEL. You collect your brother, he's older than you, he still goes to school?

KATURIAN. It's a special school. It's a learning difficulties. *(Pause.)* Is this a Jew thing? I don't know any Jews.

ARIEL. You don't know any Jews?

KATURIAN. I don't have anything *against* any Jews, but I don't *know* any Jews.

ARIEL. But you don't have anything *against* any Jews?

KATURIAN. No. Should I have?

TUPOLSKI. "Should I have?" Good answer. "Should I have?" Kind of lily-livered and subservient on the one hand, yet vaguely sarcastic and provocative on the other. "Should I have?"

KATURIAN. I wasn't trying to be provocative.

TUPOLSKI. Were you trying to be subservient?

KATURIAN. No.

TUPOLSKI. Then you were trying to be provocative. And now Ariel is going to hit you again ...

KATURIAN. Listen, I don't understand what I'm doing here. I don't know what you want me to say. I don't have anything against anybody. Any Jews or you or anybody. I just write stories. That's all I do. That's my life. I stay in and I write stories. That's it. *(Ariel stands, moves to the door.)*

ARIEL. This reminds me. I'm going to talk to the brother. *(Ariel exits, Tupolski smiles.)*

KATURIAN. *(Stunned, scared.)* My brother's at school.

TUPOLSKI. Me and Ariel, we have this funny thing, we always say, "This reminds me" when the thing hasn't really reminded us of the thing we're saying it reminds us of at all. It's really funny.

KATURIAN. My brother's at school.

TUPOLSKI. Your brother is one door down.

KATURIAN. *(Pause.)* But he'll be scared ...

TUPOLSKI. You seem a little scared yourself.

KATURIAN. I *am* a little scared.

TUPOLSKI. What are you scared about?

KATURIAN. I'm scared my brother is all alone in a strange place, and I'm scared your friend is gonna go kick the shit out of him, and I'm scared he's gonna come kick the shit out of me again although if he does it's okay, I mean I'd rather he didn't but if there's something in these stories you don't like then go ahead and take it out on me, but my brother gets frightened easily, and he doesn't understand these things and he's got nothing to do with these stories anyway, I've only ever read them to him, so I just think it's completely unfair you should've brought him down here and I think you should just fucking go and fucking let him out of here right now! Right fucking now!

TUPOLSKI. *(Pause.)* I bet you're all adrenaline now, aren't you, all "Ooh just shouted at a policeman," all "Ooh probably shouldn't've but ooh got really angry." Ooh. Calm the fuck down. Alright? Do you think we're animals?

KATURIAN. No.

12

TUPOLSKI. Well, we're not animals. We *deal*, sometimes, with animals. We're not animals. *(Pause.)* Your brother will be fine. I give you my word. *(Tupolski looks at another story from the pile.)* "The Tale of the Three Gibbet Crossroads." This does not have your theme, it seems.

KATURIAN. What theme?

TUPOLSKI. Y'know, your theme, "Some poor little kid gets fucked up." Your theme.

KATURIAN. That isn't a theme. Some of them have come out that way. That isn't a theme.

TUPOLSKI. Although maybe, in an oblique way, it *does* have your theme.

KATURIAN. I don't have themes. I've written, what, four hundred stories, and maybe ten or twenty have children in?

TUPOLSKI. Have *murdered* children in.

KATURIAN. So, what, this is about stories with murdered children in? Do you think I'm trying to say, "Go out and murder children"?

TUPOLSKI. I'm not saying you're trying to say "Go out and murder children." *(Pause.)* Are you trying to say, "Go out and murder children"?

KATURIAN. No! No bloody way! Are you kidding? I'm not trying to say anything at all! That's my whole thing.

TUPOLSKI. I know, I know, your whole thing, the first duty of a storyteller is to ...

KATURIAN. Yes ...

TUPOLSKI. ... Blah blah blah, I know. This "Three Gibbet Crossroads" ...

KATURIAN. If there are children in them, it's incidental. If there is politics in them, it's incidental. It's *accidental.*

TUPOLSKI. Except, the thing is, don't interrupt me when I'm talking ...

KATURIAN. No, I'm sorry ...

TUPOLSKI. If I ask you something outright, or if I go with my eyes, like, "Go ahead and say something," like with my eyes, then you go ahead and say something, but if I'm in the middle of something ...

KATURIAN. I know, I'm sorry ...

TUPOLSKI. And you're fucking doing it again! Did I ask you something outright?! Did I go with my eyes like, "Go ahead and say something"?!

KATURIAN. No.

TUPOLSKI. No, I didn't, did I? *(Pause.)* Did I? See, that *was* an outright question and I *did* go with my eyes like, "Go ahead and say something."

KATURIAN. I'm sorry. I'm nervous.

TUPOLSKI. You have a right to be nervous.

KATURIAN. I know.

TUPOLSKI. No, you didn't hear me. I said, "You have a *right* ... to be nervous."

KATURIAN. Why?

TUPOLSKI. *(Pause.)* "The Three Gibbet Crossroads." What are you trying to tell us in this story?

KATURIAN. I'm not trying to tell you anything. It's supposed to be just a puzzle without a solution.

TUPOLSKI. And what *is* the solution?

KATURIAN. *(Pause.)* There isn't one. It's a puzzle *without* a solution.

TUPOLSKI. *I* think there's a solution. But then, I'm really clever.

KATURIAN. Well, I mean, you're right, the idea is you should wonder what the solution is, but the truth is there is no solution, because there *is* nothing worse, is there? Than the two things it says.

TUPOLSKI. There is nothing worse?

KATURIAN. *(Pause.)* Is there?

TUPOLSKI. *(Paraphrases through the story.)* A man wakes up in the iron gibbet he's been left to starve to death in. He knows he *was* guilty of the crime they put him in there for, but he cannot remember what the crime was. Across the crossroads from him are two other gibbets; there's a placard outside one that reads "Rapist," there's a placard outside the second that reads "Murderer." There's a dusty skeleton inside the rapist's cage; there's a dying old man inside the murderer's cage. Our man can't read the placard outside his *own* cage, so he asks the old man to read it for him, to find out what he's done. The old man looks at the placard, looks at our man, then spits in his face in disgust. *(Pause.)* Some nuns come along. They say prayers over the dead rapist. Uh-huh. They give food and water to the old murderer. Uh-huh. They read our man's crime. The life drains from them and they walk away in tears. *(Pause.)* A highwayman comes along, ah-hah. He looks over the rapist without much interest. He sees the old murderer, smashes the lock off his cage, sets him free. He comes to our man's cage, reads his crime. The highwayman smiles slightly. Our man smiles back, slightly. The highwayman raises his gun and shoots him through the heart. As our man is dying he screams out, "Just tell me what I've done?!" The highwayman rides off without telling him what he's done. The last words that our man ever says are, "Will I go to Hell?" And the last sound he ever hears is the highwayman quietly laughing.

KATURIAN. That's a good story. That's something-esque. What kind of "esque" is it? I can't remember. I don't really go in for that "esque" sort of stuff anyway, but there's nothing wrong with that story. Is there?

TUPOLSKI. No, there's nothing wrong with that story. There's nothing in that story you would say the person who wrote this story is a sick fucking scummy cunt. No. All this story is to me, this story is a pointer.

KATURIAN. A pointer?

TUPOLSKI. It is a pointer.

KATURIAN. Oh.

TUPOLSKI. It is saying to me, on the surface I am saying this, but underneath the surface I am saying this other thing.

KATURIAN. Oh.

TUPOLSKI. It is a pointer. You understand?

KATURIAN. Yes. It is a pointer.

TUPOLSKI. It is a pointer. *(Pause.)* It's your best story, you say?

KATURIAN. No. It's *one* of my best stories.

TUPOLSKI. Oh, it's *one* of your best stories. You have so many.

KATURIAN. Yes. *(Pause.)* My best story is "The Town on the River" one. "The Tale of the Town on the River."

TUPOLSKI. Your best story is "The Tale of the Town on the River"? Wait, wait, wait, wait, wait, wait, wait, wait … *(Tupolski quickly finds the story.)* Hang on … Here we are. Ah-hah. This tells me something, "This is your best story."

KATURIAN. Why, what is it, is it a pointer? *(Tupolski stares at him.)* Um, it's the only one that was published.

TUPOLSKI. We know it's the only one that was published.

KATURIAN. So far.

TUPOLSKI. *(Half-laughs. Pause.)* The Libertad it was published.

KATURIAN. Yes.

TUPOLSKI. *The Libertad.*

KATURIAN. I don't read it.

TUPOLSKI. You don't read it.

KATURIAN. I send the stories around, you know, just in the hopes, to wherever might take them. I don't read all the …

TUPOLSKI. You don't read *The Libertad.*

KATURIAN. No.

TUPOLSKI. It isn't illegal, you read *The Libertad*.

KATURIAN. I know. Nor if you have a story published in it. I know.

TUPOLSKI. It has your theme. *(Pause.)* Did they give you themes, *The Libertad*? Like, "Write a story about a pony," or, "Write a story about some little kid who gets totally fucked up." Did they do that?

KATURIAN. They just gave a word-count thing. The maximum words.

TUPOLSKI. It was a theme of your own choosing?

KATURIAN. It was a theme of my own choosing. *(Tupolski hands Katurian the story.)*

TUPOLSKI. Read it to me.

KATURIAN. The whole of it?

TUPOLSKI. The whole of it. Standing. *(Katurian stands.)*

KATURIAN. This feels like school, somehow.

TUPOLSKI. Mm. Except at school they didn't execute you at the end. *(Pause.)* Unless you went to a really fucking tough school. *(Pause, then Katurian reads the story, enjoying his own words, its details and its twists.)*

KATURIAN. *(Pause.)* Um, "Once upon a time in a tiny cobble-streeted town on the banks of a fast-flowing river, there lived a little boy who did not get along with the other children of the town; they picked on and bullied him because he was poor and his parents were drunkards and his clothes were rags and he walked around barefoot. The little boy, however, was of a happy and dreamy disposition, and he did not mind the taunts and the beatings and the unending solitude. He knew that he was kind-hearted and full of love and that someday someone somewhere would see this love inside him and repay him in kind. Then, one night, as he sat nursing his newest bruises at the foot of the wooden bridge that crossed the river and led out of town, he heard the approach of a horse and cart along the dark, cobbled street, and as it neared he saw that its driver was dressed in the darkest of robes, the black hood of which bathed his craggy face in shadow and sent a shiver of fear through the little boy's body. Putting his fear aside, the boy took out the small sandwich that was to be his supper that night and, just as the cart was about to pass onto and over the bridge, he offered it up to the hooded driver to see if he would like some. The cart stopped, the driver nodded, got down and sat beside the little boy for a while, sharing the sandwich and discussing this and that. The driver asked the boy why he was barefoot and ragged and all alone, and as the boy told the driver of his poor, hard life, he eyed the back of the driver's cart; it was piled high with small, empty animal cages, all foul-smelling and dirt-lined, and just as the boy was about to ask what kind of animals it was had been inside them, the driver stood up and announced that he had to be on his way. "But before I go," the driver whispered, "because you have been so kindly to an old weary traveller in offering half of your already meagre portions, I would like to give you something now, the worth of which today you may not realise, but one day, when you are a little older, perhaps, I think you will truly value and thank me for. Now close your eyes." And so the little boy did what he was told and closed his eyes, and from a secret inner pocket of his robes the driver pulled out a long, sharp and shiny meat cleaver, raised it high in the air and brought it scything down onto the boy's right foot, severing all five of his muddy little toes. And as the little boy sat there in gaping silent shock, staring blankly off into the distance at nothing in particular, the driver gathered up his bloody toes, tossed them away to the gaggle of rats that had begun to gather in the gutters, got back onto his cart, and quietly rode on over the bridge, leaving the boy, the rats, the river and the darkening town of *Hamelin* far behind him." *(Looks at Tupolski for any response, giving him back the story, sitting back down.)* Of *Hamelin,* see?

TUPOLSKI. Of Hamelin.

KATURIAN. Do you get it? The little boy is the little crippled boy who can't keep up when the Pied Piper comes back to take all the children away. That's how he was crippled.

TUPOLSKI. I know that.

KATURIAN. It's a twist.

TUPOLSKI. I know it's a twist.

KATURIAN. It's the children he was after.

TUPOLSKI. It's the children who was after?

KATURIAN. It's the children the Pied Piper was after. To begin with. My idea was he *brought* the rats. He *brought* the rats. He knew the townspeople wouldn't pay. It was the children he was after in the first place.

TUPOLSKI. *(Nods. Pause.)* This reminds me. *(Goes to the filing cabinet, takes out a metal box the size of a biscuit tin, then sits back down with it, placing it on the table between them.)*

KATURIAN. What? Oh, "This reminds you." When it hasn't reminded you of anything. *(Tupolski stares at him.)* What's in the box? *(Sound of a man screaming hideously a few rooms away. Katurian stands,*

17

becoming flustered.) That's my brother.

TUPOLSKI. *(Listening.)* Yes, I believe it is.

KATURIAN. What's he doing to him?

TUPOLSKI. Well, something fucking horrible. I don't know, do I?

KATURIAN. You said you wouldn't touch him.

TUPOLSKI. I haven't touched him.

KATURIAN. But you said he would be fine. You gave me your word. *(The screaming stops.)*

TUPOLSKI. Katurian. I am a high-ranking police officer in a totalitarian fucking dictatorship. What are you doing taking my word about anything? *(Ariel returns, wrapping his bloodied hand in white cloth.)*

KATURIAN. What have you done to my brother? *(Ariel motions Tupolski over. They confer in a corner a while, then sit.)* What have you done to my brother, I said?!

TUPOLSKI. See, Ariel? Katurian's asking the questions now. First it was, "What's in the box?" — that was while you were torturing the spastic — then it's, "What have you done to my brother?"

KATURIAN. Fuck "What's in the box." What have you done to my brother?!

TUPOLSKI. Well, Ariel had a problem childhood, see, and he tends to take it out on all the retards we get in custody. It's bad, really, if you think about it.

KATURIAN. What have you done to him?!

ARIEL. Y'know, you being such an upstart and shouting all over the place, I would usually have smashed your face in by now, but because I've just been doing that to your subnormal brother, my hand really hurts, so for now I'm just going to let you off with a very stern warning.

KATURIAN. I want to see my brother. Right now.

TUPOLSKI. You smashed his face in, did you, Ariel? Except, hang on, that could be classified as police brutality, couldn't it? Oh no!

ARIEL. He really hurt my hand.

TUPOLSKI. Look at your poor hand!

ARIEL. I know, it really hurts.

TUPOLSKI. How many times have I told you? Use a truncheon, use a whaddyacall. Your bare hands, Ariel? And on a spastic? He won't even get the benefit.

KATURIAN. He's just a child!

ARIEL. I'm taking a breather now, but the next time I go in there, I think I am going to put something sharp up inside him and then turn it.

TUPOLSKI. Oh, Ariel, that'd definitely be classed as "police brutality."

KATURIAN. I want to see my brother right now!

TUPOLSKI. What happened to the third child?

KATURIAN. What? *(Pause.)* What third child?

ARIEL. So it's you and your brother, yeah? You're close, you and your brother?

KATURIAN. He's all I've got.

ARIEL. You and your spastic brother.

KATURIAN. He's not spastic.

TUPOLSKI. "The Writer and his Spastic Brother." Title for a story, Katurian.

KATURIAN. *(Tearfully.)* He's just a child.

TUPOLSKI. No, he's not. You know who was? Andrea Jovacovic was. You know who she was?

KATURIAN. *(Pause. Sitting down.)* Only from the papers.

TUPOLSKI. Only from the papers. What do you know about her, "only from the papers"?

KATURIAN. She was the girl they found on the heath.

TUPOLSKI. She was the girl they found on the heath, yes. You know how she died?

KATURIAN. No.

TUPOLSKI. Why don't you know how she died?

KATURIAN. The papers didn't say.

TUPOLSKI. The papers didn't say. You know who Aaron Goldberg was?

KATURIAN. Only from the papers.

TUPOLSKI. Yes. He was the boy they found in the dump behind the Jewish quarter. You know how he died?

KATURIAN. No.

TUPOLSKI. No, the papers didn't say. The papers didn't say a lot of things. The papers didn't say anything about the third child, a little mute girl, went missing three days ago, the same area, the same age.

ARIEL. The papers will be saying something tonight.

TUPOLSKI. The papers will be saying something tonight. The papers will be saying a lot of things tonight.

KATURIAN. About the mute girl?

TUPOLSKI. About the mute girl. About confessions. About executions. All that type of stuff.

KATURIAN. But ... I don't understand what you're trying to say

19

to me. Are you trying to say I shouldn't write stories with child-killings in because in the real world there are child-killings?

ARIEL. He wants us to think that he thinks that all we've got against him is a disagreement with his fucking prose style. Like we don't know what his brother just said to me.

KATURIAN. What did my brother just say to you?

ARIEL. Like we don't know what's in this box.

KATURIAN. Whatever he said to you, you made him say to you. He doesn't speak to strangers.

ARIEL. *(Adjusting bloodied cloth.)* He spoke to me. He speaks to strangers alright. He said you *and* he speak to strangers.

KATURIAN. I want to see him.

ARIEL. You want to see him?

KATURIAN. I want to see him. That's what I said.

ARIEL. You are demanding to see him?

KATURIAN. I would like to see my brother.

ARIEL. You are demanding to see your brother?

KATURIAN. I *am* fucking demanding, yes. I wanna see he's alright.

ARIEL. He will never be alright.

KATURIAN. *(Standing.)* I've got a right to see my brother!

ARIEL. You've got no fucking rights ...

TUPOLSKI. Sit down, please.

ARIEL. Not no more, you've got no rights.

KATURIAN. I've got rights. Everybody's got rights.

ARIEL. You ain't.

KATURIAN. Why ain't I?

TUPOLSKI. Open the box.

KATURIAN. Huh?

ARIEL. I'll give you your rights in a minute.

KATURIAN. Yeah, like I bet you gave my brother his rights too.

ARIEL. I gave him his rights alright.

KATURIAN. I bet you did. I bet you fucking did.

TUPOLSKI. Open the box.

ARIEL. No, *I* bet I fucking did.

KATURIAN. Yeah, I bet you fucking did.

ARIEL. No, *I* bet I fucking did!

KATURIAN. I know you bet you fucking did…!

TUPOLSKI. *(Screaming.)* Open the fucking box!!!

KATURIAN. I'll open the fucking box! *(Katurian angrily wrenches the box's lid off, then recoils in horror at what's inside, shivering in a corner.)* What's that?

TUPOLSKI. Retake your seat, please.

KATURIAN. What are they? *(Ariel darts over, drags Katurian back to his seat and, holding him by the hair, forces him to look into the box.)*

ARIEL. "What are they?" You know what they are. We found them in your house.

KATURIAN. No...!

ARIEL. Your brother's already admitted his part ...

KATURIAN. No!

ARIEL. But he's hardly the brains behind the operation. You know how the girl on the heath died? Two razor blades down her little fuck-ing throat, both wrapped in apple, funnily enough. *(Tupolski reaches into the box ...)* You know how the little Jew boy died? (... *and pulls out five bloody toes.)*

TUPOLSKI. His first toe, his second toe, his third toe, his fourth toe, his fifth toe.

ARIEL. That poor little Jew boy's five fucking toes and they were found in your house and it's nothing to do with you?

KATURIAN. *(Crying.)* I just write stories!

ARIEL. They make a nice final fucking twist, don't they?

TUPOLSKI. Make him swallow them. *(Ariel wrenches Katurian off the chair.)*

ARIEL. Where's the mute girl?! Where's the mute girl?! *(Ariel tries to force the toes into Katurian's mouth.)*

TUPOLSKI. Don't make him swallow them, Ariel. What are you doing?

ARIEL. You *said* make him swallow them.

TUPOLSKI. Only to scare him! They're evidence! Have *some* sense!

ARIEL. Fuck off "Have some sense"! Don't start on me again! And quit it with that "problem childhood" shit too.

TUPOLSKI. But you *did* have a problem childhood ...

ARIEL. Quit it, I said!

TUPOLSKI. And look at your hand, that's so obviously fake blood.

ARIEL. Oh, fuck off!

TUPOLSKI. Pardon me?

ARIEL. I said, "Fuck off!" *(Ariel tosses the toes on the floor and exits moodily. Tupolski gathers up the toes, puts them back in the box.)*

TUPOLSKI. So moody. *(Pause.)*

KATURIAN. I don't understand a thing that's going on.

TUPOLSKI. No? Well here's where we stand as of five-fifteen P.M., Monday the fourth. Along with the evidence we found in your house, your brother, spastic or not, has, under duress or not, admitted enough about the killings for us to execute him before the evening's out, but, as Ariel said, he's hardly the brains behind the operation, so we want you to confess too. We like executing writers. Dimwits we can execute any day. And we do. But, you execute a writer, it sends out a signal, y'know? *(Pause.)* I don't know what signal it sends out, that's not really my area, but it sends out a signal. *(Pause.)* No, I've got it. I know what signal it sends out. It sends out the signal "DON'T … GO … AROUND … KILLING … LITTLE … FUCKING … KIDS." *(Pause.)* Where's the mute girl? Your brother didn't seem to want to spill the beans.

KATURIAN. Detective Tupolski?

TUPOLSKI. Mister Katurian?

KATURIAN. I've listened to your bullshit for a long time now, and I want to tell you a couple of things. I don't believe my brother said a word to you. I believe that you are trying to frame us for two reasons. One, because for some reason you don't like the kind of stories I write, and two, because for some reason you don't like retarded people cluttering up your streets. I also believe that I'm not going to say another word to you until you let me see my brother. So torture me as much as you like, Detective Tupolski, 'cos I ain't saying another fucking word.

TUPOLSKI. *(Pause.)* I see. *(Pause.)* Then I'd best go get the electrodes. *(Tupolski exits with the metal box. Door clicks shut behind him. Katurian's head slumps. Blackout.)*

Scene 2

Katurian, sitting on a bed amongst toys, paints, pens, paper, in an approximation of a child's room, next door to which there is another identical room, perhaps made of glass, but padlocked and totally dark. Katurian narrates the short story which he and the Mother, in diamonds, and Father, in a goatee and glasses, enact.

KATURIAN. Once upon a time there was a little boy upon whom his mother and father showered nothing but love, kindness, warmth, all that stuff. He had his own little room in a big house in the middle of a pretty forest. He wanted for nothing: All the toys in the world were his; all the paints, all the books, paper, pens. All the seeds of creativity were implanted in him from an early age and it was writing that became his first love: short stories, fairy tales, little novels, all happy, colourful things about bears and piglets and angels and so forth, and some of them were good, some of them were very good. His parents' experiment had worked. The *first part* of his parents' experiment had worked. *(The Mother and Father, after caressing and kissing Katurian, enter the adjoining room, and leave our sight.)* It was the night of his seventh birthday that the nightmares first started. The room next door to his own room had always been kept bolted and padlocked for reasons the boy was never quite sure of but never quite questioned until the low whirring of drills, the scritchety-scratch of bolts being tightened, the dull fizz of unknown things electrical, and the muffled screams of a small gagged child began to emanate through its thick brick walls. On a nightly basis. *(To Mother, in a boy's voice.)* "What were all those noises last night, Mama?" *(Normal voice.)* he'd ask, after each long, desperate, sleepless night, to which his mother would ever reply …

MOTHER. Oh little Kat, that's just your wonderful but overactive imagination playing tricks on you.

KATURIAN. *(Boy's voice.)* Oh. Do all little boys of my age hear such sounds of abomination nightly?

MOTHER. No, my darling. Only the extraordinarily talented ones.

KATURIAN. *(Boy's voice.)* Oh. Cool. *(Normal voice.)* And that was that. And the boy kept on writing, and his parents kept encouraging him with the utmost love, but the sounds of the whirrs and screams kept going on … *(In the nightmare semi-dark of the adjoining room, it appears for a second as if a child of eight, strapped to the bed, is being tortured with drills and sparks.)* … and his stories got darker and darker and darker. They got better and better, due to all of the love and encouragement, as is often the case, but they got darker and darker, due to the constant sound of child-torture, as is also often the case. *(Light in the adjoining room fades out. The Mother, Father and child can no longer be seen. Katurian clears all the toys, etc., away.)* It was on the day of his fourteenth birthday, a day he was waiting to hear the results of a story competition he was short-listed for, that a note slipped out from under the door of the locked room … *(A note in red writing slips under door. Katurian picks it up.)* … a note which read: "They have loved you and tortured me for seven straight years

23

for no reason other than as an artistic experiment, an artistic experiment which has worked. You don't write about little green pigs anymore, do you?" The note was signed "Your brother," and the note was written in blood. *(Katurian axes into the next-door room.)* He axed through the door to find ... *(Lights rise on Mother and Father alone in room, with drills and taped noises as described.)* ... his parents sitting in there, smiling, alone; his father doing some drill noises; his mother doing some muffled screams of a gagged child; they had a little pot of pig's blood between them, and his father told him to look at the other side of the blood-written note. The boy did, and found out he'd won the fifty-pounds first prize in the short-story competition. They all laughed. The second part of his parents' experiment was complete. *(The Mother and Father lie down to sleep side by side on Katurian's bed. Lights fade on them.)* They moved house soon after that and though the nightmare sounds had ended, his stories stayed strange and twisted but good, and he was able to thank his parents for the weirdness they'd put him through, and years later, on the day that his first book was published, he decided to revisit his childhood home for the first time since he'd left. He idled around his old bedroom, and all the toys and paints still littered around there ... *(Katurian enters the adjoining room, sits on the bed.)* ... then he went into the room beside it that still had the old dusty drills and padlocks and electrical cord lying around, and he smiled at the insanity of the very idea of it all, but he lost his smile when he came across ... *(The bed feels terribly lumpy. He pulls the mattress off to reveal the horrific corpse of a child ...)* ... the corpse of a fourteen-year-old child that had been left to rot in there, barely a bone of which wasn't broken or burned, in whose hand there lay a story, scrawled in blood. And the boy read that story, a story that could only have been written under the most sickening of circumstances, and it was the sweetest, gentlest thing he'd ever come across, but, what was even worse, it was better than anything he himself had ever written. Or ever would. *(Katurian takes a lighter and sets the story alight.)* So he burnt the story, and he covered his brother back up, and he never mentioned a word of what he had seen to anybody. Not to his parents, not to his publishers, not to anybody. The final part of his parents' experiment was over. *(Lights fade in adjoining room, but rise slightly on the bed where his Mother and Father are still lying.)* Katurian's story "The Writer and the Writer's Brother" ended there in fashionably downbeat mode, without touching upon the equally downbeat but somewhat more self-incrimimating details of the truer story, that after he'd read the blood-written note and broken into the next-door room it was, of course ... *(The child's corpse sits bolt upright in bed, breathing heavily.)* ... his brother he found in there, alive, as such, but brain-damaged beyond repair, and that that night, whilst his parents were sleeping, the fourteen-year-old birthday boy held a pillow over his father's head for a little while ... *(Katurian suffocates his Father with a pillow. His body spasms, then dies. He taps his Mother on the shoulder. She opens her sleepy eyes to see her open-mouthed dead husband.)* ... and, after waking her a moment just to let her see her dead blue husband, he held a pillow over his mother's head for a little while, too. *(Katurian, face blank, holds a pillow over his screaming Mother's head. Her body spasms wildly, but he forcefully keeps the pillow down, as the lights slowly fade to black.)*

End of Act One

ACT TWO

Scene 1

A cell. Michal sitting on a wooden chair, tapping his thighs, listening to the intermittent screams of his brother, Katurian, being tortured a room away. A blanket on a thin mattress and a pillow lie a few yards away.

MICHAL. "Once upon a time ... a long long way away ... " *(Katurian screams again. Michal mimics them at length, till they fade away.)* "Once upon a time, a long long way away, there was a little green pig. There was a little green pig. Who was green. Um ... " *(Katurian screams again. Michal mimics till they fade, then gets up, idles around.)* "Once upon a time, a long long way away, there was a little green pig ... " Or *was* it a long long way away? Where was it? *(Pause.)* Yes, it *was* a long long way away, and he was a little green pig ... *(Katurian screams. Michal mimics, irritated this time.)* Oh shut up, Katurian! Making me forget the little green pig story now with your screaming all over the place! *(Pause.)* And what did the little green pig do next? He ... he said to the man ... He said to the man, "Hello ... Man ... " *(Katurian screams. Michal just listens.)* Ah, I can't do stories like you do stories, anyway. I wish they'd hurry up and stop torturing ya. I'm bored. It's boring in here. I wish ... *(Sound of next-door room being unbolted. Michal listens. Michal's cell is unbolted and the bloody, breathless Katurian is thrown in by Ariel.)*
ARIEL. We'll be back to work on you in a minute. I'm getting my dinner. *(Michal gives him the thumbs-up. Ariel bolts the door behind him. Michal looks over Katurian, who is shivering on the floor, goes to caress his head, can't quite do it, and sits on the chair.)*
MICHAL. Hiya. *(Katurian looks up at him, crawls over and hugs Michal's leg. Michal stares down at him, feeling awkward.)* What are you doing?
KATURIAN. I'm holding on to your leg.
MICHAL. Oh. *(Pause.)* Why?

KATURIAN. I don't know, I'm in pain! Aren't I allowed to hold on to my brother's leg when I'm in pain?

MICHAL. Of course you are, Katurian. Just seems weird.

KATURIAN. *(Pause.)* How are you doing, anyway?

MICHAL. Great. Just a bit bored. Cor, you were making some racket. What were they doing, torturing ya?

KATURIAN. Yeah.

MICHAL. *(Tuts. Pause.)* Did it hurt? *(Katurian lets go of Michal's leg.)*

KATURIAN. If it didn't hurt, Michal, it wouldn't be torture, would it?

MICHAL. No, I suppose.

KATURIAN. Did yours hurt?

MICHAL. Did my what hurt?

KATURIAN. When they tortured you.

MICHAL. They didn't torture me.

KATURIAN. What? *(Katurian looks him over for the first time, seeing there are no cuts or bruises.)*

MICHAL. Oh, no, the man said he was *going* to torture me, but I thought, "No way, boy, that'd hurt," so I just told him whatever he wanted to hear, and he was fine then.

KATURIAN. But I heard you scream.

MICHAL. Yes. He asked me to scream. He said I did it really good.

KATURIAN. So he just told you what to say and you agreed to it?

MICHAL. Yeah.

KATURIAN. *(Pause.)* Swear to me on your life that you didn't kill those three kids.

MICHAL. I swear to you on my life that I didn't kill those three kids. *(Katurian breathes a sigh of relief, hugging Michal's leg again.)*

KATURIAN. Did you sign anything?

MICHAL. Huh? You know I can't sign nothing.

KATURIAN. Then maybe we can still get out of this.

MICHAL. Get out of what?

KATURIAN. Get out of being executed for killing three children, Michal.

MICHAL. Oh, get out of being executed for killing three children. That'd be good. How?

KATURIAN. The only thing they've got against us is what you've said, and the stuff they said they found in the house.

MICHAL. What stuff?

KATURIAN. They had this box full of toes. No, hang on. They *said* they were toes. They didn't look *that* much like toes. They

27

could've been anything. Shit, man. *(Pause.)* And they said they'd tortured you too, his hands were all covered in blood. Are you saying he didn't touch you at all?

MICHAL. No, he gave me a ham sandwich. Except I had to take the lettuce out. Yeah.

KATURIAN. Let me think for a minute. Let me think for a minute ...

MICHAL. You like thinking, don't ya?

KATURIAN. Why are we being so stupid? Why are we believing everything they're telling us?

MICHAL. Why?

KATURIAN. This is just like storytelling.

MICHAL. I know.

KATURIAN. A man comes into a room, says, "Your mother's dead," yeah?

MICHAL. I know my mother's dead.

KATURIAN. No, I know, but in a story. A man comes in to a room, says to another man, "Your mother's dead." What do we know? Do we know that the second man's mother is dead?

MICHAL. Yes.

KATURIAN. No, we don't.

MICHAL. No, we don't.

KATURIAN. All we know is that a man has come into a room and said to another man, "Your mother is dead." That is all we know. First rule of storytelling. "Don't believe everything you read in the papers."

MICHAL. I don't read the papers.

KATURIAN. Good. You'll always be one step ahead of everybody else.

MICHAL. I think I'm pretty sure I don't know what you're going on about, Katurian. But you're funny, though.

KATURIAN. A man comes into a room, says, "Your brother's just confessed to the killing of three children and we found one of the kid's toes in a box in your house." What do we know?

MICHAL. Aha! I get it!

KATURIAN. Do we know that the brother has killed three children?

MICHAL. No.

KATURIAN. No. Do we know that the brother has *confessed* to killing three children?

MICHAL. No.

KATURIAN. No. Do we know that they found a kid's toes in a

28

box in their house? No. Do we ... Oh my God ...

MICHAL. What?

KATURIAN. We don't even know that there were any children killed at all.

MICHAL. It was in the papers.

KATURIAN. Who runs the papers?

MICHAL. The police. Ohh. You're quite clever.

KATURIAN. Oh my God. "A writer in a totalitarian state is interrogated about the gruesome content of his short stories and their similarities to a number of child-murders that are happening in his town. A number of child-murders ... that aren't actually happening at all." *(Pause.)* I wish I had a pen now. I could do a decent story out of this. If they weren't going to execute us in an hour. *(Pause.)* Whatever they do, Michal, no matter what, you don't sign anything. No matter what they do to you, you don't sign anything. You got it?

MICHAL. Whatever they do to me, I don't sign anything. No matter what they do to me, I don't sign anything. *(Pause.)* Can I sign *your* name?

KATURIAN. *(Smiling.) Especially* don't sign my name. *Especially* don't sign my name.

MICHAL. "I killed a loada kids," signed Katurian Katurian. Hah!

KATURIAN. You little shit ...

MICHAL. "And it was nothing to do with his brother, Michal, not even a bit," signed Katurian Katurian. Hah!

KATURIAN. I'll beat the shit out of ya ...

MICHAL. Don't ... *(Katurian hugs him. Michal hugs back, too strongly on Katurian's wounds.)*

KATURIAN. Arrghh, *Jesus*, Michal!

MICHAL. Sorry, Katurian.

KATURIAN. It's alright. *(Pause.)* We'll be alright, Michal. We'll be alright. We'll get out of here. If we just stick together.

MICHAL. Yeah. My arse is really itchy today. I don't know why. Have we got any of that powder left?

KATURIAN. No, you used it all. Like it was going out of style.

MICHAL. Mm. But we ain't going home for a while anyway, are we?

KATURIAN. No.

MICHAL. Gonna have to sit here with an itchy arse then.

KATURIAN. Yeah, but could you keep telling me about it, because it's really keeping my spirits up.

MICHAL. My, really? No, you're just being stupid. You can't have an arse keep your spirits up, can ya?

29

KATURIAN. It depends on the arse.

MICHAL. What? Stupid. *(Pause.)* Well it's itchy anyway. I'll tell you that. I'm trying not to itch it or anything, y'know, 'cos you're here, but, I'll tell ya, it's itchy, man. *(Pause.)* I've got one itchy arse. *(Pause.)* Tell us a story, Katurian. It'll take my mind off …

KATURIAN. Take your mind off your itchy arse …

MICHAL. My itchy arse, yeah …

KATURIAN. What story do you want?

MICHAL. Um, "The Little Green Pig."

KATURIAN. No. Thatsh justh thilly …

MICHAL. It'sh not justh thilly, it's good, "The Little Green Pig." I was trying to r'member it just now.

KATURIAN. No, I'll do a different one. What'll I do?

MICHAL. Do "The Pillowman."

KATURIAN. *(Smiles.)* Why "The Pillowman"? *(Michal shrugs.)* Jeez, that's from a while ago, isn't it?

MICHAL. Yeah, it's from, like, a while ago.

KATURIAN. Let's see, how does that start…?

MICHAL. "Once upon a time" …

KATURIAN. I know, but I'm trying to think how it actually starts …

MICHAL. *(Irritated.)* "Once upon a time" …

KATURIAN. Alright, *Jesus. (Pause.)* Once upon a time … there was a man, who did not look like normal men. He was about nine feet tall … *(Michal looks up, silently whistles.)* And he was all made up of these fluffy pink pillows: His arms were pillows and his legs were pillows and his body was a pillow; his fingers were tiny little pillows, even his head was a pillow, a big round pillow.

MICHAL. A *circular* pillow.

KATURIAN. It's the same thing.

MICHAL. But I prefer "a *circular* pillow."

KATURIAN. His head was a circular pillow. And on his head he had two button eyes and a big smiley mouth which was always smiling, so you could always see his teeth, which were also pillows. Little white pillows.

MICHAL. "Pillows." Do your mouth smiley like the Pillowman's mouth is. *(Katurian gives a big dopey smile. Michal gently touches Katurian's lips and cheeks.)*

KATURIAN. Well, the Pillowman had to look like this, he had to look soft and safe, because of his job, because his job was a very sad and a very difficult one …

MICHAL. Uh-oh, here it comes …

30

KATURIAN. Whenever a man or a lady was very very sad because they'd had a dreadful and hard life and they just wanted to end it all, they just wanted to take their own lives and take all the pain away, well, just as they were about to do it, by razor, or by bullet, or by gas, or ...

MICHAL. Or by jumping off of something big.

KATURIAN. Yes. By whatever preferred method of suicide — "preferred"'s probably the wrong word, but anyway, just as that person was about to do it, the Pillowman would go to them, and sit with them, and gently hold them, and he'd say, "Hold on a minute," and time would slow strangely, and as time slowed, the Pillowman would go back in time to when that man or that lady was just a little boy or a little girl, to when the life of horror they were to lead hadn't quite yet begun, and the Pillowman's job was very very sad, because the Pillowman's job was to get that child to kill themselves, and so avoid the years of pain that would just end up in the same place for them anyway: facing an oven, facing a shotgun, facing a lake. "But I've never heard of a small child killing themselves," you might say. Well, the Pillowman would always suggest they do it in a way that would just look like a tragic accident: He'd show them the bottle of pills that looked just like sweeties; he'd show them the place on the river where the ice was too thin; he'd show them the parked cars that it was really dangerous to dart out between; he'd show them the plastic bag with no breathing holes, and exactly how to tighten it. Because mummies and daddies always find it easier to come to terms with a five-year-old lost in a tragic accident than they do with a five-year-old who has seen how shitty life is and taken action to avoid it. Now, not all the children would go along with the Pillowman. There was one little girl, a happy little thing, who just wouldn't believe the Pillowman when he told her that life could be awful and her life would be, and she sent him away, and he went away crying, crying big gloopy tears that made puddles this big, and the next night there was another knock on her bedroom door, and she said, "Go away, Pillowman. I've told you, I'm happy. I've *always been* happy and I'll *always be* happy." But it wasn't the Pillowman. It was another man. And her mummy wasn't home, and this man would visit her every time her mummy wasn't home, and she soon became very very sad, and as she sat in front of the oven when she was twenty-one she said to the Pillowman, "Why didn't you try to convince me?" And the Pillowman said, "I tried to convince you, but you were just too

31

happy." And as she turned on the gas as high as it would go she said, "But I've *never* been happy. I've *never* been happy."

MICHAL. Um, could you skip on to the end, please? This bit's a bit boring.

KATURIAN. Well, that's a bit rude, Michal, actually.

MICHAL. Oh. Sorry, Katurian. *(Pause.)* But could you skip on to the end please?

KATURIAN. *(Pause.)* Well … the end of the Pillowman … See, when the Pillowman was successful in his work, a little child would die horrifically. And when the Pillowman was unsuccessful, a little child would have a horrific life, grow into an adult who'd also have a horrific life, and *then* die horrifically. So, the Pillowman, as big as he was and as fluffy as he was, he'd just go around crying all day long, his house'd be just puddles everywhere, so he decided to do just one final job and that'd be it. So he went to this place beside this pretty stream that he remembered from a time before …

MICHAL. I like this bit …

KATURIAN. And he brought a little can of petrol with him, and there was this old weeping willow tree there, and he went under it and he sat and he waited there a while, and there were all these little toys under there, and …

MICHAL. Say what the toys was.

KATURIAN. There was a little car there, and a little toy dog and a kaleidoscope.

MICHAL. There was a little toy dog?! Did it yap?

KATURIAN. Did it what?

MICHAL. Did it yap?

KATURIAN. Er … yes. Anyway, there was a little caravan nearby, and the Pillowman heard the door open and little footsteps come out, and he heard a boy's voice say, "I'm just going out to play, Mum," and the mum said, "Well don't be late for your tea, son." "I won't be, Mum." And the Pillowman heard the little footsteps get closer and the branches of the willow tree parted and it wasn't a little boy at all, it was a little Pillowboy. And the Pillowboy said, "Hello," to the Pillowman, and the Pillowman said, "Hello," to the Pillowboy, and they both played with the toys for a while …

MICHAL. With the car and the kaleidoscope and the little toy dog what yapped. But I bet mostly with the little toy dog, ay?

KATURIAN. And the Pillowman told him all about his sad job and the dead kids and all of that type of stuff, and the little Pillowboy understood instantly 'cos he was such a happy little fella and all he ever wanted to do was to be able to help people, and he poured the can of petrol all over himself and his smiley mouth was still smiling, and the Pillowman, through his gloopy.tears, said, "Thank you," to the Pillowboy, and the Pillowboy said, "That's alright. Will you tell my mummy I won't be having my tea tonight," and the Pillowman said, "Yes, I will," lying, and the Pillowboy struck a match, and the Pillowman sat there watching him burn, and as the Pillowman gently started to fade away, the last thing he saw was the Pillowboy's happy smiley mouth as it slowly melted away, stinking into nothingness. That was the last thing he saw. The last thing he heard was something he hadn't even contemplated. The last thing he heard was the screams of the hundred thousand children he'd helped to commit suicide coming back to life and going on to lead the cold, wretched lives that were destined to them because he hadn't been around to prevent them, right on up to the screams of their sad self-inflicted deaths, which this time, of course, would be conducted entirely alone.

MICHAL. Hm. *(Pause.)* I don't really get the end bit but, ah, so the Pillowman just faded away? Ah.

KATURIAN. He just faded away, yeah, like he never existed.

MICHAL. Into the air.

KATURIAN. Into the air. Into wherever.

MICHAL. Into Heaven.

KATURIAN. No. Into wherever.

MICHAL. I like the Pillowman. He's my favourite.

KATURIAN. It's a bit downbeat, I'll admit. Is your itchy arse alright now?

MICHAL. Oh, it was till you reminded me! Arrgh! *(Adjusts himself.)* Hmm. But I still can't figure it out.

KATURIAN. Figure what out? Figure out "The Pillowman"?

MICHAL. No, I thought I'd hidden it really well.

KATURIAN. Hidden what really well?

MICHAL. The box with the little boy's toes in it. I thought I'd hidden it really well. I mean, first I'd put it under all my socks and pants in the drawer, which, alright, wasn't very well hid, but then when they started to smell I hid 'em under the dirt in the Christmas tree pot in the attic, 'cos I knew we wouldn't be getting the Christmas tree pot out again for ages. Like, till Christmas. And that'd give 'em plenty of time to go mouldy. They were already a bit mouldy. Were they mouldy when you saw 'em? *(Katurian nods, the life drained out of him.)* They must've used sniffer dogs or something. You know those sniffer dogs? They must've used them. Because, no way, I hid them brilliant. Christmas tree pot. You only see it once a year.

KATURIAN. You just told me ... You just told me you didn't touch those kids. You just lied to me.

MICHAL. No I didn't. I just told you the man came in and said he'd torture me unless I said I killed those kids, so I said I killed those kids. That doesn't mean I didn't kill those kids. I did kill those kids.

KATURIAN. You swore to me, on your life, that you didn't kill those three kids.

MICHAL. Ohh. See with that one, the "Swear to me on your life you didn't kill those three kids," yeah, I was kind of playing a trick on ya. Sorry, Katurian. *(Katurian backs away from him to the mattress.)* I know it was wrong. Really. But it was very interesting. The little boy was just like you said it'd be. I chopped his toes off and he didn't scream at all. He just sat there looking at them. He seemed very surprised. I suppose you would be at that age. His name was Aaron. He had a funny little hat on, kept going on about his mum. God, he bled a lot. You wouldn't've thought there'd be that much blood in such a little boy. Then he stopped bleeding and went blue. Poor thing. I feel quite bad now, he seemed quite nice. "Can I go home to my mummy, now, please?" But the girl was a pain in the arse. Kept bawling her eyes out. And she wouldn't eat them. She wouldn't eat the applemen, and I'd spent *ages* making them. It's really hard to get the razor blades inside. You don't say how to make them in the story, do ya? I checked. So, anyway, I had to force 'em down her. It only took two. Not being mean, but at least that shut her up. *(Pause.)* It's really hard to get out of your clothes, isn't it, blood? You try washing your shirt tomorrow. It'll take ages. You'll see. *(Pause.)* Katurian? *(Pause.)* I'll wash it for ya, if you want. I'm getting quite good at it.

KATURIAN. *(Pause. Quietly.)* What did you do it for?

MICHAL. Huh? You're mumbling.

KATURIAN. *(Tears.)* What did you do it for?

MICHAL. Don't cry, Katurian. Don't cry. *(Michal goes over to hold him. Katurian backs away in disgust.)*

KATURIAN. What did you do it for?

MICHAL. *You* know. Because you told me to.

KATURIAN. *(Pause.)* Because I what?

MICHAL. Because you told me to.

KATURIAN. *(Pause.)* I remember telling you to do your home-work on time. I remember telling you to brush your teeth every night …

MICHAL. I *do* brush my teeth every night …

KATURIAN. I don't remember telling you to take a bunch of lit-tle kids and go butcher them.

MICHAL. I didn't butcher them. "Butcher them," it'd be more like … *(Michal imitates viciously hacking at someone.)* Mine was more like … *(Michal imitates a gentle, single hack onto imaginary toes, then delicately throwing the toes away …)* And … *(Michal imi-tates placing two applemen inside a little mouth, then swallowing.)* "Butcher them." That's a bit strong. And I wouldn't have done any-thing if you hadn't told me, so don't you act all the innocent. Every story you tell me, something horrible happens to somebody. I was just testing out how far-fetched they were. 'Cos I always thought some of 'em were a bit far-fetched. *(Pause.)* D'you know what? They ain't all that far-fetched.

KATURIAN. How come you never acted out any of the nice ones?

MICHAL. Because you never wrote any nice ones.

KATURIAN. I wrote plenty of nice ones.

MICHAL. Er, yeah, like, two.

KATURIAN. No, I'll tell you why you never acted out any of the nice ones, shall I?

MICHAL. Alright.

KATURIAN. Because you're a sadistic, retarded fucking pervert who *enjoys* killing little kids, and even if every story I ever wrote was the sweetest thing imaginable, the outcome'd still be the fucking same.

MICHAL. Well … we'll never know, will we, 'cos you never did. *(Pause.)* And I *didn't* enjoy killing those kids. It was irritating. It took ages. And I didn't *set out* to kill those kids. I just set out to chop the toes off one of them and to put razors down the throat of one of them.

KATURIAN. Are you telling me you don't know that if you chop the toes off a little boy and put razors down the throat of a little girl, you don't know that they're gonna die?

MICHAL. Well, I know *now. (Katurian puts his head in his hands, trying to think of a way out of this.)* Well, the torture man certainly seemed to be on my side. He seemed to agree it was all your fault. Well, mostly your fault.

KATURIAN. *(Pause.)* What did you tell him?

MICHAL. Just the truth.

KATURIAN. Which particular truth?

MICHAL. Just that, y'know, all the things I did to all the kids I got from stories you wrote and read out to me.

KATURIAN. You said that to the policeman?

MICHAL. Mm. Y'know, just the truth.

KATURIAN. That isn't the truth, Michal.

MICHAL. Yes it is.

KATURIAN. No it isn't.

MICHAL. Well, *did* you write some stories with children getting murdered in them?

KATURIAN. Yes, but ...

MICHAL. Well, *did* you read them out to me?

KATURIAN. Yes ...

MICHAL. Well, *did* I go out and murder a bunch of children? *(Pause.)* "Yes, I did," is the answer to that one. So I don't see how the "That isn't the truth" comes into it. Let alone the "statistic retarded pervert." I mean, you're my brother and I love you, but, y'know, you've just spent twenty minutes telling me a story about a bloke, his main thing in life's to get a bunch of little kids to, at minimum, set themselves on fire, so, y'know? And he's the hero! And I'm not criticising. He's a very good character. He's a very very good character. He reminds me a lot of me.

KATURIAN. How does he remind you of you?

MICHAL. You know, getting little children to die. All that.

KATURIAN. The Pillowman never killed anybody, Michal. And all the children that died were going to lead horrible lives anyway.

MICHAL. You're right, all children are going to lead horrible lives. You may as well save them the hassle.

KATURIAN. Not all children are going to lead horrible lives.

MICHAL. Erm, hmm. Did *you* lead a horrible life since you was a child? Yes. Erm, did *I* lead a horrible life since I was a child? Yes. That's two out of two for a start.

KATURIAN. The Pillowman was a thoughtful, decent man, who hated what he was doing. You are the opposite, in every respect.

MICHAL. Well, okay, you know I'm no good at opposites, but I think I know what you're saying. Thank you. *(Pause.)* "The Pillowman"'s a good story, Katurian. It's one of your best. Y'know, I think you're going to be a famous writer some day, God bless you. I can see it.

KATURIAN. *(Pause.)* When?

MICHAL. Hah?

KATURIAN. When am I going to be a famous writer?

MICHAL. *Some day,* I said.

KATURIAN. They're going to execute us in an hour and a half.

MICHAL. Oh yeah. Well, I guess you aren't gonna be a famous writer then.

KATURIAN. They're going to destroy everything now. They're going to destroy us, they're going to destroy my stories. They're going to destroy everything.

MICHAL. Well, I think it's *us* we should be worrying about, Katurian, not your stories.

KATURIAN. Oh yeah?

MICHAL. Yeah. They're just paper.

KATURIAN. *(Pause.)* They're just what?

MICHAL. They're just paper. *(Katurian thuds Michal's head down once against the stone floor. Michal, stunned by the idea of it rather than the pain, feels his bleeding head.)*

KATURIAN. If they came to me right now and said, "We're going to burn two out of the three of you — you, your brother, or your stories," I'd have them burn you first, I'd have them burn me second, and I'd have it be the stories they saved.

MICHAL. You just banged my head on the floor.

KATURIAN. I noticed that.

MICHAL. *(Crying.)* You just banged my head on the floor!

KATURIAN. I said I noticed that.

MICHAL. You're just like Mum and Dad!

KATURIAN. *(Laughing.)* Say that again?!

MICHAL. You're just like Mum and Dad! Hitting me, and shouting at me!

KATURIAN. *I'm* just like Mum and Dad? Let me work this out...

MICHAL. Oh don't start that ...

KATURIAN. Mum and Dad kept their first-born son in a room where they tortured him for seven straight years, and you made a little boy bleed to death, made a little girl choke to death, did God knows what to another little girl and *you're not* like Mum and Dad, but I banged a fucking dimwit's head on the floor once and *I am* like Mum and Dad.

MICHAL. Yes, exactly. Exactly.

KATURIAN. I see your logic, Michal. I see where you're coming from.

MICHAL. Good. You should.

KATURIAN. I'll tell you this. If Mum and Dad are looking down right now, I think they'll be glad to see you turned out to be exactly the type of boy they could be proud of.

MICHAL. Don't say that …

KATURIAN. Truly proud of. You're a carbon copy of them, almost. Maybe you should grow a little goatee beard here, get glasses, like him …

MICHAL. Don't say that!

KATURIAN. Or wear a lot of diamonds, like her. Tawlk like thiiss, my son …

MICHAL. Don't say that or I'll kill you!!!

KATURIAN. You're not gonna kill me, Michal. *I ain't seven!!!*

MICHAL. I'm not like them. I didn't want to hurt anybody. I was just doing your stories.

KATURIAN. What did you do to the third girl?

MICHAL. No, I'm not telling now. You've hurt my feelings. And my head.

KATURIAN. You'll tell quick enough when *they* get hold of you.

MICHAL. I can take it.

KATURIAN. Not like this you can't.

MICHAL. *(Low.)* You don't know what I can take.

KATURIAN. *(Pause.)* No. I suppose I don't.

MICHAL. When I was in here listening to you screaming next door, I thought this musta been kinda like how it was for you all those years. Well, let me tell ya, it's easier from this side.

KATURIAN. I know it is.

MICHAL. You only had it for an hour and you came in whinge-ing your snotty head off. Try it for a lifetime.

KATURIAN. That doesn't excuse anything.

MICHAL. It excused the two *you* murdered. Why shouldn't it excuse the two I murdered?

KATURIAN. I murdered two people who tortured a child for seven years. You murdered three children who hadn't tortured any-body for any years. There's a difference.

MICHAL. As far as *you* know they hadn't tortured anybody. The razor-blade girl seemed like a right little shit. I bet she at least did ants.

KATURIAN. How did you kill the third girl, Michal? I just need to know. Was she like in a story too?

MICHAL. Mm.

KATURIAN. Which story?

MICHAL. You're gonna be mad

KATURIAN. I'm not gonna be mad.

MICHAL. You're gonna be a bit mad.

KATURIAN. Which story was she like?

MICHAL. Like, um … she was like in, um … "The Little Jesus." "The Little Jesus." *(Katurian looks at Michal a while, hands to his face, and, as he pictures the horrific details of the story, he slowly starts to cry. Michal goes to say something but can't, as Katurian continues quietly crying.)*

KATURIAN. Why that one?

MICHAL. *(Shrugs.)* It's a good story. You're a good writer, Katurian. Don't let anybody tell you different.

KATURIAN. *(Pause.)* Where did you leave her?

MICHAL. Down where you buried Mum and Dad. At the wishing well.

KATURIAN. *(Pause.)* That poor fucking thing.

MICHAL. I know. It's terrible.

KATURIAN. Well, I hope it was quick.

MICHAL. Quickish. *(Katurian cries again. Michal puts a hand on his shoulder.)* Don't cry, Kat. It'll be alright.

KATURIAN. How will it be alright? How will it ever be alright?

MICHAL. I dunno. It's just sort of something you say at a time like this, isn't it? "It'll be alright." Course it won't be alright. They're gonna come and execute us any minute, aren't they? That isn't alright, is it? That's almost the opposite of alright. Mm. *(Pause.)* Will they execute us together or separate? I hope it's together. I wouldn't wanna be on my own.

KATURIAN. *I* haven't *done* anything!

MICHAL. Look, don't start that again or you'll get on my nerves. And even if they *don't* execute us together, they're bound to bury us together, save digging two holes, 'cos I'd hate to be buried all on my own. That'd be horrible. All alone in the ground, ierrghh! But at least we'll be together in Heaven, whatever happens. And hang out with God and that. Have races.

KATURIAN. Which particular Heaven is this you're going to, Michal? Child-killer Heaven?

MICHAL. No, not Child-killer Heaven, smart-arse. Normal Heaven. Like in the films.

KATURIAN. Do you want to know where you're going when you die?

MICHAL. Where? And don't say somewhere horrible just because you're in a mood.

KATURIAN. You're going to go to a little room in a little house in a little forest, and for the rest of all time you're going to be looked after not by me but by a person called Mum and a person called Dad, and they're gonna look after you in the same way they always looked after you, except this time I'm not gonna be around to rescue you, 'cos I ain't going to the same place you're going, 'cos I never butchered any little fucking kids.

MICHAL. That is just the most meanest thing that any person has ever said to any other person and I am never never going to speak to you again ever.

KATURIAN. Good. Then let's just sit here in silence till they come back and execute us.

MICHAL. The meanest thing I ever heard! And I *told* you not to say anything mean. I said, "Don't say anything mean," and what did you do? What did you do? You went and said something mean.

KATURIAN. I used to love you so much.

MICHAL. *(Pause.)* What do you mean, "used to"? That's an even meaner thing to say than the other mean thing you said, and that other thing was the meanest thing I ever heard! Jesus!

KATURIAN. Then let's just sit here in silence.

MICHAL. I'm *trying* to sit here in silence. You keep saying mean stuff. *(Pause.)* Don't ya? *(Pause.)* Don't ya, I said? Oh, is this the sitting here in silence thing? Okay. *(Pause. Michal scratches his arse. Pause.)* Except I've got another bone to pick with you, actually. A bone which is all about this little rubbish story I read a little while ago. A little rubbish story called "The Writer and the Writer's Brother," the story was called, which was the biggest pile of rubbish I ever read.

KATURIAN. I never showed you that story, Michal.

MICHAL. I know you never showed me that story. And with good reason. It was rubbish.

KATURIAN. So you've been snooping round my room while I'm at work, have you?

MICHAL. Of course I've been snooping round your room while you're at work. What the hell do you think I do while you're at work?

KATURIAN. Massacre infants, I thought.

MICHAL. Uh-huh? Well, when I'm not massacring infants I'm snooping around your room. And finding stupid little stories that aren't even true at the end. That are just bloody stupid at the end. That I died and Mum and Dad lived. That's a bloody stupid ending.

KATURIAN. Now I'm getting literary advice from Jack-the-fucking-Ripper.

MICHAL. Why didn't you make it a happy ending, like it was in real life?

KATURIAN. There are no happy endings in real life.

MICHAL. What? My story was a happy ending. You came and rescued me and you killed Mum and Dad. That was a happy ending.

KATURIAN. And then what happened?

MICHAL. Then you buried them out behind the wishing well, and put some limes on them.

KATURIAN. I put *lime* on them. "Put some limes on them." What was I doing, a fruit fucking salad? And then what happened?

MICHAL. And then what happened? And then you started sending me to school and then I started learning things, which was good.

KATURIAN. And then what happened?

MICHAL. And then what happened? *(Pause.)* When I won the discus?

KATURIAN. And then what happened about three weeks ago?

MICHAL. Oh. And then I done some children in.

KATURIAN. And then you done some children in. How is that a happy fucking ending? And then you got caught and executed, and got your brother executed, who hadn't done anything at all. How is that a happy ending? And, hang on, when did you win the discus? You came *fourth* in the fucking discus!

MICHAL. We're not talking about …

KATURIAN. You came fourth out of fucking *four* in the discus! "When I won the discus."

MICHAL. We're not talking about did I win the discus or not, we're talking about what would be a happy ending! Me winning the discus, that would be a happy ending, see? Me dead and left to rot, like in your stupid story, that would not be a happy ending.

KATURIAN. That *was* a happy ending.

MICHAL. *(Almost tearful.)* What? That I am dead and left to rot, that's a happy ending?

KATURIAN. What was left in your hand when you died? A story. A story that was better than any of *my* stories. See, "The Writer and the Writer's Brother" … *you* were the writer. *I* was the writer's brother. That made it a happy ending for you.

MICHAL. But I was dead.

KATURIAN. It isn't about being or not being dead. It's about what you leave behind.

MICHAL. I don't get it.

KATURIAN. Right at this moment, I don't care if they kill me. I

41

don't care. But they're not going to kill my stories. They're not going to kill my stories. They're all I've got.

MICHAL. *(Pause.)* You've got me. *(Katurian just looks at him a moment, then looks down sadly. Michal turns away tearfully.)* But, okay, so we agree you're going to change the end of the "Writer and his Brother" story and have me alive at the end and Mum and Dad are dead and I win the discus. That's okay, then. And you should probably just burn the old story really just so's nobody sees it and thinks it's the proper story and that I'm dead or something. Should probably just burn it.

KATURIAN. Okay, Michal, I'll do that.

MICHAL. Really?

KATURIAN. Really.

MICHAL. Wow. Cool. That was easy. Well, y'know, in that case, there's probably a lot more of your stories you should burn too, 'cos some of 'em, and I'm not being funny or anything, but some of 'em are a bit sick, really.

KATURIAN. Why don't we just burn all of them, Michal. It'd save a lot of time weeding out the sick ones from the not-sick ones.

MICHAL. No, no, that'd be silly, burning all of them. No. Just the ones that are gonna make people go out and kill kids. And it wouldn't take long weeding out the ones that *aren't* gonna make people go out and kill kids, 'cos you've only got about two that *aren't* gonna make people go out and kill kids, haven't ya?

KATURIAN. Oh really, yeah?

MICHAL. Yeah.

KATURIAN. And which ones would they be? Which ones, out of the four hundred stories I've written would you deign to save?

MICHAL. Well, the one about the little green pig, that's a nice one. That wouldn't make anybody go out and murder anybody, rea-ally ... and ... *(Pause.)* And ... *(Pause.)* I suppose that's about it, actually. "The Little Green Pig" one.

KATURIAN. That's about it?

MICHAL. Yeah. I mean, if you want to be on the safe side. I mean, you've got some that'd probably make somebody go out and *maim* somebody, not actually *kill* them, but, y'know, if you want to be on the safe side, it's just "The Little Green Pig" one. It might make someone go out and paint somebody green, or something, hah! But that's about it.

KATURIAN. This would all be fine, if it wasn't for the fact that the three stories you chose to act out just happened to be the three

42

most repulsive stories you *could've* chosen to act out. They weren't the first three you happened to come across, they were the three that most suited your repulsive little mind.

MICHAL. So, what, I could've done ones that wouldn't've been so horrible? Like what? Like "The Face Basement"? Slice off their face, keep it in a jar on top of a dummy, downstairs? Or "The Shakespeare Room"? Old Shakespeare with the little black pygmy lady in the box, gives her a stab with a stick every time he wants a new play wrote?

KATURIAN. He didn't do all those plays himself.

MICHAL. But you see what I mean, Kat? They're all sick. You couldn't've picked one that wouldn't've been just as sick.

KATURIAN. Why did it have to be "The Little Jesus," though?

MICHAL. Ah Katurian, what's done is done and can't never be undone. Ta-dun! 'Cos I'm getting a bit sleepy now so I'm gonna have a little sleep for myself if I can just get my mind off my arse which is still itchy like crazy and I haven't even mentioned it.

(Michal settles down on the mattress.)

KATURIAN. You're going to sleep?

MICHAL. Mm.

KATURIAN. But they're coming back to torture and execute us any minute.

MICHAL. Exactly, so it might be the last sleep we get for a while. *(Pause.)* Might be the last sleep we get ever. Wouldn't that be terrible? I love sleeping. Do you think they have sleeping in Heaven? They bloody better, else I'm not going. *(Pause.)* Katurian?

KATURIAN. What?

MICHAL. Tell me a story.

KATURIAN. I thought you wanted to burn all my stories.

MICHAL. Tell me the one about the little green pig. I don't wanna burn that one, tell me that one. And then I'll forgive you.

KATURIAN. Forgive me for what?

MICHAL. Forgive you for saying those mean things that Mum and Dad would be in charge of me for all time in the little forest and no one would ever come rescue me.

KATURIAN. *(Pause.)* I can't remember how it goes, "The Little Green Pig" …

MICHAL. You remember how it goes, Katurian, come on. The first word goes "once," the second word goes "upon." I think the third word goes "a," and the fourth word goes … oh sugar, what's the fourth word?

KATURIAN. You're a little smart-arse, aren't you?

43

MICHAL. Uh, "time," the fourth word goes, I just remembered. "Once upon a time ... "

KATURIAN. Okay. Settle down ... *(Michal does so, the pillow beside his head.)* Once upon a time ...

MICHAL. This is like the olden days. The *good* olden days. Stories ...

KATURIAN. Once upon a time, on a farm in a strange land, far away ...

MICHAL. Far away ...

KATURIAN. There lived a little pig who was different from all the other pigs around.

MICHAL. He was green.

KATURIAN. Are you telling this story or am I?

MICHAL. You. Sorry. Fingers on lips. Shh.

KATURIAN. He was different from all the other pigs, because he was bright green. Like, almost glow-in-the-dark green.

MICHAL. Glow-in-the-dark green. Like the paint they have in the railway tunnels, that's the glow-in-the-dark like they have in the railway tunnels?

KATURIAN. Yes.

MICHAL. Yes.

KATURIAN. Now are we interrupting or are we listening and sleeping?

MICHAL. We are listening and sleeping.

KATURIAN. Good. Now, the little pig, he really liked being green. Not that he didn't like the colour of normal pigs, he thought pink was nice too, but what he liked was, he liked being a little bit different, a little bit peculiar. The other pigs around him didn't like him being green, though. They were jealous and they bullied him and made his life a misery...

MICHAL. A misery ...

KATURIAN. And all this complaining just aggravated the farmers, and they...

MICHAL. What's "aggravated?" Sorry, Katurian.

KATURIAN. It's alright. It just means it got on their nerves.

MICHAL. *(Yawning.)* Got on their nerves ...

KATURIAN. It got on the nerves of the farmers and they thought, "Hmm, we'd better do something about this." So, one night, as all the pigs lay sleeping out in the open fields, they crept out and snatched up the little green pig and brought him back to the barn, and the little pig was squealing and all the other pigs were just

44

laughing at him ...

MICHAL. *(Quietly.)* Bastards ...

KATURIAN. And when the farmers got him to the barn, what they did was they opened up this big pot of this very special pink paint and they dunked him in it till he was covered from head to foot and not a patch of green was left, and they held him down until he dried. And what was special about this pink paint was it could never be washed off and it could never be painted over. It could never be washed off and it could never be painted over. And the little green pig said — *(Piggy voice.)* "Oh please God, please don't let them make me like all the rest. I'm happy in being a little bit peculiar."

MICHAL. "I'm happy in being a little bit peculiar," he says to God.

KATURIAN. But it was too late, the paint was dry, and the farmers sent him back out into the fields, and all the pink pigs laughed at him as he passed and sat down on his favourite little patch of grass, and he tried to understand why God hadn't listened to his prayers, but he couldn't understand, and he cried himself to sleep, and even all the thousand tears he cried couldn't help wash off the horrible pink paint, because ...

MICHAL. It could never be washed off and it could never be painted over.

KATURIAN. Exactly. And he went to sleep. But that night, as all the pigs in the fields lay a-sleeping, these strange, strange storm clouds began to gather overhead and it began to rain, slowly at first but getting heavier and heavier and heavier. But this was no ordinary rain, this was a very special *green* rain, almost as thick as paint and not only that, there was something else special about it. It could never be washed off and it could never be painted over. It could never be washed off ... *(Katurian looks in on Michal. He's asleep. Katurian keeps the rest of the story to a low whisper.)* ... and it could never be painted over. And when morning came and the rain had stopped and all the pigs awoke, they found that every single one of them had turned bright green. Every single one except, of course, the old little green pig, who was now the little pink pig, upon whom the strange rain had washed right off because of the unpaintoverable paint the farmers had covered him in earlier. "Unpaintoverable." *(Pause.)* And as he looked at the strange sea of green pigs that lay around him, most of which were crying like babies, he smiled, and he thanked goodness, and he thanked God, because he knew that he was still, and he always would be, just a little bit peculiar. *(Pause. Katurian listens to the sleeping Michal a while, stroking his hair gently.)*

You like that one, don't you, Michal? *(Pause.)* You used to like that one. No little toes in it … no razor blades in it. It's nice. *(Pause.)* Maybe you should've acted out that one. *(Pause.)* It's not your fault, Michal. It's not your fault. *(Pause. Crying.)* Sweet dreams, little baby. I'll be coming along soon. *(Katurian takes the pillow and holds it down forcefully over Michal's face. As Michal starts to jerk, Katurian sits across his arms and body, still holding the pillow down. After a minute Michal's jerks lessen. After another minute he's dead. Once Katurian is certain of this, he takes the pillow off, kisses Michal on the lips, crying, and closes his eyes. He goes to the door, clangs it loudly.)* Detectives?! *(Pause.)* Detectives?! I would like to make a confession to my part in the murders of six people. *(Pause.)* I have one condition. *(Pause.)* It involves my stories. *(Blackout. Interval.)*

Scene 2

Katurian narrates the story that the girl and the parents act out. Slight costume change from nice parents to foster-parents, played by the same couple.

KATURIAN. Once upon a time in a land not so very far away there lived a little girl, and, although this little girl's gentle parents hadn't brought her up very religiously at all, she was quite quite determined that she was the second coming of the Lord Jesus Christ. *(Girl puts on a very false beard and a pair of sandals and starts blessing things, etc.)* Which was somewhat strange for any six-year-old. She'd wear a little beard and would go around in sandals, blessing stuff. She could be forever found walking amongst the poor and the homeless, consoling the drunks and the drug addicts, and generally consorting with the type of person her mummy and daddy didn't deem suitable for a six-year-old to be consorting with. Each time they would drag her home from some unsavoury sort she would stamp and scream and throw her dollies about, and when her parents would counter that …
PARENTS. Jesus never stamped and screamed and threw his dollies about …
KATURIAN. She'd reply, "That was the *old* Jesus! Get it?" Well,

one day, the little girl slipped away yet again, and for two horrify-
ing days her parents could find neither hide nor hair of her, until
they received a distraught call from a priest they didn't know, saying, "You'd better come down to the church. Your daughter's here
giving us a lot of shit. It was cute at first but now it's really getting
irritating." *(Lights slowly fade on smiling nice parents.)* Well, her parents didn't care about all that, they were just relieved that she was
alive and well, and they sped downtown to pick her up, but in their
haste they careened into an oncoming meat truck, were beheaded
and died. *(Lights fully out on nice parents as they bleed.)* The little girl
was informed of the news; she cried one single tear, and not a single tear more, as she thought Jesus would've done if he'd lost his
parents in a vehicular beheading; and she was shipped off by the
state to live in a forest with some abusive foster-parents ... *(Enter
the evil foster-parents, who take the girl by the hand, holding it too
tightly.)* ... who hadn't informed the state that they were abusive on
the form; who hated religion, who hated Jesus, who hated anybody,
in fact, who didn't hate anybody, and who, as would follow, hated
the little girl. *(Foster-parents whip off her beard and throw it away.)*
She bore their hate with a happy heart and forgave them, but this
didn't seem to work. When she insisted on attending church of a
Sunday, they took her sandals away, forcing her to walk there barefoot and alone, over craggy roads of broken glass, yet when she got
there she'd kneel for hours, praying for her Father in Heaven to forgive them, only to get told off for bleeding all over the church.
She'd receive a beating for arriving late home, though no time had
been set for her arrival; she'd receive a beating for sharing her food
with the poor children at school, she'd receive a beating for cheer-
ing up the ugly kids, she'd receive a beating for wandering about
looking for lepers. Her life was a constant torture, yet she bore it
with a smile and it all only made her stronger, till this one day
when she met a blind man begging by the roadside ... *(Katurian
plays the blind man. She rubs dust and spittle over his eyelids.)* She
mixed a little of her spittle in the dust and rubbed it over his eyes.
He reported her to the police for rubbing dust and spittle in his
eyes, and when her foster-parents got her back from the police sta-
tion they said to her ...
FOSTER PARENTS. So you want to be just like Jesus, do you?
KATURIAN. And she said, *"Finally* you fucking get it!" *(Pause.)*
And they stared at her a little while. And then it started. *(The
dreadful details of the following are all acted out onstage.)* Her foster-

mother embedded in her daughter's head a crown of thorns made of barbed wire, because she was too lazy to make a proper crown of thorns, while her foster-father whipped her with a cat-o'-nine tails, and after an hour or two of that, they asked her, when she regained consciousness …

FOSTER PARENTS. Do you still want to be like Jesus?

KATURIAN. And, through her tears, she said, "Yes, I do." *(The parents place a heavy cross on the girl's back. She walks around with it in pain.)* So they made her carry a heavy wooden cross around the sitting room a hundred times until her legs buckled and her shins broke and she could do nothing but stare at her little legs going the wrong way, and they said to her …

FOSTER PARENTS. Do you still want to be like Jesus?

KATURIAN. And she almost got sick for a second, but she swallowed it so she wouldn't look weak and she looked them in the eye and she said, "Yes, I do." *(The parents nail her to the cross and stand it upright.)* And then they nailed her hands to the cross and bent her legs back around the right way and nailed her feet to the cross and they stood the cross up against the back wall and left her there while they watched television, and when all the good programmes were over they turned it off and they sharpened a spear and they said to her …

FOSTER PARENTS. Do you still want to be like Jesus?

KATURIAN. And the little girl swallowed her tears and she took a deep breath and she said, "No. I don't want to be like Jesus. I fucking *am* Jesus!" *(Pause.)* And her parents stuck the spear in her side … *(They do so.)* … and they left her there to die, and they went to bed. *(The little girl's head slowly bows, eyes closing. Morning light, foster parents return.)* And in the morning they were quite surprised that she wasn't dead … *(Girl slowly opens her eyes, nods a hello. They gently take her down off the cross. She touches their faces as if she has forgiven them. They place her in a glass coffin and seal the lid.)* … so they took her down off the cross and they buried her alive in a little coffin with just enough air to live for three days … *(They shovel dirt onto the coffin lid.)* … and the last voices she heard were her foster parents above, calling out …

FOSTER PARENTS. Well, if you're Jesus, you'll rise again in three days, won't you?

KATURIAN. And the little girl thought about it for a while, then she smiled to herself and she whispered, "Exactly. Exactly." *(Pause.)* And she waited. And she waited. And she waited. *(Lights fade on the coffin somewhat, as the girl, slowly, scrapes her fingernails down the lid. Katurian walks up to and over it.)* Three days later a man out walking the woods stumbled over a small, freshly dug grave, but, as the man was quite quite blind, he carried on by, sadly not hearing a horrible scratching of bone upon wood a little way behind him, that ever so slowly faded away and was lost forever in the black, black gloom of the empty, empty, empty forest. *(Blackout.)*

End of Act Two

ACT THREE

Police interrogation room. Katurian hurriedly writing out a lengthy confession. He hands the first page to the seated Tupolski. Ariel is standing, smoking.

TUPOLSKI. "I hereby confess to my part in the murders of six people; three carried out by me alone, three carried out by myself and my brother while acting out a number of gruesome and perverted short stories I had written." Brackets, "Attached," close brackets. *(Pause.)* "My most recent killing was that of my brother, Michal ... " Yeah, thanks for that, Katurian. We'd never've been able to pin that one on you. "Held a pillow over his head ... " blah blah blah ... "save him the horror of torture and execution at the hands of his ... " blah blah blah. Stuff about how much he loves his brother. Yeah, you really showed it. "My most recent killing prior to that was of a little mute girl, about three days ago. I do not know her name. This little girl ... was ... "

ARIEL. *(Pause.)* This little girl was what?

TUPOLSKI. It's the end of the page.

ARIEL. Write quicker.

TUPOLSKI. Write quicker. *(Pause.)* Or is it "write *more quickly*"? "Write quicker." "Write more quickly."

ARIEL. It's "write quicker" ...

TUPOLSKI. It's "write quicker." *(Ariel cricks his neck, reading upside down what Katurian is writing. Katurian, almost instinctively, covers what he's writing with his hand. Ariel slaps him across the head.)*

ARIEL. You're not doing your fucking exams!

KATURIAN. I'm sorry ... *(Ariel reads over Katurian's shoulder.)*

ARIEL. "Killed as we acted out a story called ... 'The Little Jesus.' " Which one's "The Little Jesus"? I didn't see that one ...

TUPOLSKI. What? *(Ariel flips through the box file, finds "The Little Jesus" story.)*

ARIEL. He says they killed her like a story called "The Little Jesus." Did *you* see that one?

TUPOLSKI. *(Sickened, sad.)* Yes. I did. *(Ariel starts reading through the story. Katurian glances at Tupolski and is disturbed by his stare. He gives him the second page of the confession and continues writing.)* Where did you leave her body?

KATURIAN. I've drawn a map. There's a wishing well about two hundred yards behind our house in the Kamenice forest. Right behind that wishing well, her body's buried there. With two other people. Two adults.

TUPOLSKI. What two other people?

KATURIAN. I'm getting to that. *(Tupolski checks his gun. Katurian notices but continues writing.)*

TUPOLSKI. *(To Ariel.)* Where are you up to?

ARIEL. "She'd wear a little beard and would go around in sandals."

TUPOLSKI. Ariel, if you're reading a story to find out how a child got murdered, wouldn't it be an idea just to skip to the end of it?

ARIEL. Oh. Right.

TUPOLSKI. Like, skip to the bit about the crown of thorns. Or skip to the bit about the cat-o'-nine-tails. Or skip to the bit about the "carrying a crucifix around the room until her legs fucking buckled." Or skip to the bit right after that. *(Pause.)* I'll get them to send out the forensics people, pick up the body. *(Tupolski exits with Katurian's map. Ariel finishes the story and starts quietly crying. Katurian looks at him, then continues with the confession. Ariel sits, sickened.)*

ARIEL. Why does there have to be people like you? *(Katurian finishes the page, continues on another. Ariel reads through the first page.)* "And I held him down as my brother cut his toes off, acting out a story called 'The Tale of the Town on the River.' Attached." *(Pause.)* "And I held her down, as he fed her a number of little figures made from apples, with razor blades inside them, acting out a story called 'The Little Apple Men.' Attached." *(Pause.)* Do you really think we're not going to burn every one of your stories the minute we kill you?

KATURIAN. I've confessed to everything truthfully, just like I promised I would. And I believe that you'll keep all my stories with my case file and not release them until fifty years after my death, just like you promised you would.

ARIEL. What makes you think we'll keep our word?

KATURIAN. Because I think, deep down, you're honourable men.

ARIEL. *(Standing, seething.)* Deep down?! Deep fucking down…?!

KATURIAN. Could you beat me up after I've finished this? I'm just up to the part about murdering my mother and father. *(Katurian continues writing. Ariel lights a cigarette.)* Thank you.

ARIEL. *(Pause.)* You killed your mum and dad? *(Katurian nods.)* This may seem a ridiculous question, but, er, why?

KATURIAN. Um ... There's a story in there called "The Writer and the Writer's Brother." I don't know if you saw it ...

ARIEL. I saw it.

KATURIAN. Well ... I kind of hate any writing that's even vaguely autobiographical. I think people who only write about what they know only write about what they know because they're too fucking stupid to make anything up, however "The Writer and the Writer's Brother" is, I suppose, the only story of mine that isn't really fiction.

ARIEL. Oh. *(Pause.)* How old was he? When they started.

KATURIAN. He was eight. I was seven.

ARIEL. How long did it go on for?

KATURIAN. Seven years.

ARIEL. And you heard it all those years?

KATURIAN. I didn't know exactly what it was, till the end, but yes.

ARIEL. And then you killed them? *(Katurian nods, handing the finished confession to Ariel.)*

KATURIAN. I held a pillow over each of their heads, then I buried them behind the wishing well behind our house. I thought the wishing well was kind of apt. Anyway, it's the same place where the mute girl's buried. *(Ariel goes over to the filing cabinet, checks inside.)*

ARIEL. Y'know, your childhood could be used as a pretty decent defence in court. Well, it could if we weren't going to bypass all that court shit and shoot you in an hour.

KATURIAN. I don't want to bypass anything. I just want you to keep your word. To go ahead and kill me, and to go ahead and keep my stories safe.

ARIEL. Well, you can certainly half-trust us.

KATURIAN. I can trust you.

ARIEL. How do you know you can trust me?

KATURIAN. I don't know. There's just something about you. I don't know what it is.

ARIEL. Oh, really? Well, y'know, I'll tell you what there is about me. There is an overwhelming, and there is an all-pervading, hatred ... a hatred ... of people like you. Of people who lay even the littlest finger ... on children. I wake up with it. It wakes me up. It rides on the bus with me to work. It whispers to me, "They will not get away with it." I come in early. I make sure all the bindings are clean and the electrodes are in the right order so we won't ...

waste ... time. I admit it, sometimes I use excessive force. And sometimes I use excessive force on an entirely innocent individual. But I'll tell you this. If an entirely innocent individual leaves this room for the outside world, they're not gonna contemplate even raising their *voice* to a little kid again, just in case *I* fucking hear 'em and drag 'em in here for *another* load of excessive fucking force. Now, is this kind of behaviour in an officer of the law in some way questionable morally? Of course it fucking is! But you know what? I don't fucking care! 'Cos, when I'm an old man, you know what? Little kids are gonna follow me around and they're gonna know my name and what I stood for, and they're gonna give me some of their sweets in thanks, and I'm gonna take those sweets and thank them and tell them to get home safe, and I'm gonna be happy. Not because of the sweets, I don't really like sweets, but because I'd know ... I'd know in my heart, that if I hadn't been there, not all of them would have been there. Because I'm a good policeman. Not necessarily good in the sense of being able to solve lots of stuff, because I'm not, but good in the sense of I stand for something. I stand for something. I stand on the right side. *I* may not always be right, but I stand on the right side. The child's side. The opposite side to you. And so, naturally, when I hear that a child has been killed in a fashion ... in a fashion such as this "Little Jesus" thing ... You know what? I would torture you to death just for *writing* a story like that, let alone acting it out! So, y'know what? *(Takes out from the cabinet a large, grim-looking battery and electrodes.)* ... Fuck what your mum and dad did to you and your brother. Fuck it. I'd've tortured the fuck out of them if I had them here, just like I'm gonna torture the fuck out of you now too. 'Cos two wrongs do not make a right. Two wrongs do not make a right. So kneel down over here, please, so I can connect you to this battery. *(Katurian backs away.)*

KATURIAN. Come on, not again ...

ARIEL. Come over here, please, I said ... *(Tupolski enters.)*

TUPOLSKI. What's going on?

ARIEL. I'm just about to connect him to this battery.

TUPOLSKI. Jesus, what kept you?

ARIEL. We were talking.

TUPOLSKI. What about?

ARIEL. Nothing.

TUPOLSKI. Were you doing your "Children are gonna come up and give me sweets when I'm an old man" speech?

ARIEL. Fuck. You.

TUPOLSKI. *(Taken aback.)* Pardon me? That's the second time today you've …

ARIEL. *(To Katurian.)* You! Kneel down here, please. I've already asked you politely. *(Katurian slowly goes over to Ariel. Tupolski sits at the desk, scans through the rest of the confession. Katurian kneels down.)*

KATURIAN. And who was the first one who told *you* to kneel down, Ariel? Your mum or your dad? *(Ariel stops dead still. Tupolski's jaw drops.)*

TUPOLSKI. Fuck me.

KATURIAN. I'm guessing your dad, right?

TUPOLSKI. Oh you didn't go and tell him all your dad shit, did you, Ariel? Jesus!

ARIEL. No, Tupolski, I didn't go and tell him all my dad shit.

TUPOLSKI. What? Oh. Shit. That old one.

ARIEL. *(To Tupolski.)* You keep chipping away with that shit, don't you? With that "problem childhood" shit?

TUPOLSKI. I don't keep chipping away with anything. You're the one keeps bringing your problem childhood up.

ARIEL. I've never said a word about my problem childhood. I wouldn't *use* the phrase "problem childhood" to describe my childhood.

TUPOLSKI. What phrase would you use? A "fucked by your dad" childhood? That isn't a phrase. *(Ariel starts shaking slightly.)*

ARIEL. Would you like to give the prisoner any further information, Tupolski?

TUPOLSKI. I'm just tired of everybody round here using their shitty childhoods to justify their own shitty behaviour. *My* dad was a violent alcoholic. Am I a violent alcoholic? Yes I am, but that was my *personal choice.* I freely admit it.

ARIEL. I would like to get back to torturing the prisoner now.

TUPOLSKI. Get back to torturing the prisoner now. You've kept him waiting ages. *(Ariel connects electrodes to Katurian as he speaks.)*

ARIEL. You've overstepped the mark today, Tupolski.

TUPOLSKI. I am reading through the prisoner's confession, Ariel, to ensure we've left no aspects of this case unaccounted for. I'm doing my job. I'm not torturing a condemned fuckwit just to satisfy my own sadist vengeance fantasies.

ARIEL. Way overstepped the mark.

TUPOLSKI. Hurry up and torture the prisoner, please, Ariel. We've got to shoot him in half an hour. *(Ariel connects the electrodes to the battery.)*

KATURIAN. Where's your father now, Ariel?

ARIEL. Do not say a word, Tupolski! Do not say a word!

TUPOLSKI. I'm not saying a word. I'm reading his confession. I'm doing my job. Like I say.

KATURIAN. Is he in prison?

ARIEL. And you shut your mouth also, pervert.

KATURIAN. Or you'll do what? Or you'll torture and execute me? *(Pause.)* Is he in prison?

ARIEL. Shh shh shh, I'm trying to concentrate ...

TUPOLSKI. He's not in prison, no.

ARIEL. What did I just actually say?

KATURIAN. They never arrested him?

TUPOLSKI. They *couldn't* arrest him.

ARIEL. Tupolski! It would be very bad for all concerned to continue with this ... with this line of conversation.

TUPOLSKI. I have a dreadful feeling you're right.

ARIEL. So I will just connect this last electrode up here, and I will just connect this last electrode up here ...

KATURIAN. Why couldn't they arrest him?

ARIEL. Shh shh shh ...

KATURIAN. Why couldn't they arrest him? *(Ariel has cleared himself from the electrodes and is just about to turn the battery on when Tupolski, at the last possible moment, speaks.)*

TUPOLSKI. Because Ariel had already murdered him, of course. *(Ariel laughs slightly, shaking again. He doesn't turn the battery on.)* Well, it wasn't really murder, was it? More like self-defence, diminished responsibility, all that. I call it murder just to tease him. Hey, *I'd* murder *my* dad if he crawled into bed with me every week from the age of eight, y'know? *(Pause.)* Mm. He held a pillow over his head while he was sleeping. I see you boys have a lot in common. *(Tupolski flattens the confession out on the table. Pause.)*

ARIEL. I am going to speak to the Commandant now, and I am going to inform him of your behaviour throughout this investigation. It has been lacking in focus and in clarity from the start. From the start. Such as what was that whole "peripheral vision" thing? That whole "peripheral vision at the bottom of your eyes" thing? What was all that about?

TUPOLSKI. Disconcert and destabilise the prisoner with asinine nonsense, it's in all the guidebooks, Ariel. I would like now to continue questioning the prisoner without the aid of your electrical claptrap, so could you disconnect Mr. Katurian, if you don't mind, I'd like him to focus.

ARIEL. And I shall ask the Commandant to have me replace you as the Number One on this investigation because this isn't the first time this has happened, is it, and the Commandant likes me and he has said so and Number Ones have been replaced before, and you will be reprimanded, and the conclusion of this case will be tied up by me. The tying up of all the loose ends of this case will be tied up by me. I will be the one to tie them up.

TUPOLSKI. And what would your first step be in the tying up of this case?

ARIEL. Well, as I was *trying* to do, before you came in and *said* all those things, my first step would be to torture the prisoner with the aforesaid electricity, wasn't it?

TUPOLSKI. Why?

ARIEL. Why? Because he killed those fucking kids!

TUPOLSKI. See, *my* first step would be to ask him a number of questions pertaining to the killing of the mute girl.

ARIEL. Uh-huh?

TUPOLSKI. My first question would be, "Is it true, Mr. Katurian … " I'd say it like that, sort of formal. "Is it true, Mr. Katurian, that you and your brother, in acting out 'The Little Jesus' story, at one point placed a crown of thorns on that little girl's head?"

KATURIAN. Yes, it is true.

TUPOLSKI. It is true. My second question would be, "Was this before or after you whipped her with a cat-o'-nine-tails?"

KATURIAN. After.

ARIEL. We know all this.

TUPOLSKI. My third question would be, "Did you then make her walk around a while carrying a heavy wooden cross, which you then proceeded to crucify her upon?"

KATURIAN. Yes, we did that.

TUPOLSKI. You did that. Did you then, to top it all, stick a big fucking spear in her pretty little side?

KATURIAN. Yes, we did. I'm ashamed.

TUPOLSKI. And did you then bury this girl?

KATURIAN. Yes.

ARIEL. I said we know all this.

TUPOLSKI. In the story itself, the little girl is still alive when she's buried. Was the little mute girl still alive when you buried her, or was she dead?

KATURIAN. *(Pause.)* What?

TUPOLSKI. Was the little mute girl still alive when you buried her, or was she dead? *(Katurian gropes for an answer, but doesn't have one.)*

KATURIAN. *(Quietly.)* I don't know.

TUPOLSKI. Pardon me?

KATURIAN. I don't know.

TUPOLSKI. You don't know. You don't know if she was alive or if she was dead. Um, Ariel? On the way to your friend the Commandant, could you call the search team, get them to hurry it up a bit, just in case it's a live little mute girl we're getting them to dig up? Thanks, babe. *(Ariel looks at him a moment, then dashes out of the room. Tupolski idles over to the kneeling Katurian and the battery.)* How can you not know?

KATURIAN. It was hard to tell. She wasn't breathing that much. I *think* she was dead. I *think* she was. She's got to be by now, hasn't she? After all that?

TUPOLSKI. Has she? Has she got to be? I don't know. I've never crucified a child then buried her in a coffin. I don't know. *(Tupolski starts fiddling with the battery wires. Katurian braces himself for the shock. Tupolski disconnects the electrodes and returns to his seat.)* I'd *assume* she's dead. I'd *assume*. But I don't know. It just struck me as I was telling the forensics boys. All you said was you acted out "The Little Jesus." That might be alright for Ariel. "Sorry, Officer, I did it." Bzzz! That's not alright for me. See, Ariel's a policeman. He polices. Police dogs can police. I'm a detective. I, sometimes, like to detect.

KATURIAN. I'm sure she's dead.

TUPOLSKI. Not sure enough though, ay? *(Pause.)* I wrote a little story once, y'know. It sort of summed up my world view, in some ways. Well, no, it didn't really sum up my world view. I don't have a world view. I think the world's a pile of shit. That isn't really a world view, is it? Or is it? Hmmm. *(Pause.)* Anyway, I wrote this little story once, and … hang on, alright, no, if it doesn't sum up my world view, it sums up my view of detective work and the relation of that detective work to the world at large. That's it, yeah. Why are you still kneeling down?

KATURIAN. I don't know.

TUPOLSKI. It just looks stupid.

KATURIAN. Yes. *(Tupolski gestures to the chair. Katurian takes the final electrodes off and sits in the chair.)*

TUPOLSKI. So, do you want to hear my story?

KATURIAN. Yes.

TUPOLSKI. Well, you wouldn't say no, would you?

KATURIAN. No.

TUPOLSKI. No. Well, my story is called ... What's it called? It's called ... "The Story of the Little Deaf Boy on the Big Long Railroad Tracks. In China." *(Pause.)* What?

KATURIAN. What?

TUPOLSKI. Don't you think that's a good title?

KATURIAN. I *do* think that's a good title, yes.

TUPOLSKI. *(Pause.)* What do you really think? You have my permission to be entirely truthful, even if it hurts me.

KATURIAN. I think that's probably about the worst title I ever heard. It's got about two commas in it. You can't have two commas in a title. You can't have *one* comma in a title. It might even have a full stop in it, that title. That title's almost insane.

TUPOLSKI. *(Pause.)* Maybe it's a title that's just way ahead of its time.

KATURIAN. Maybe it is. Maybe terrible titles *are* way ahead of their time. Maybe that'll be the new thing.

TUPOLSKI. Maybe it will.

KATURIAN. I just think it's a terrible title.

TUPOLSKI. We've established that! I'm taking back my permission to be entirely truthful now and you're lucky you don't get a fucking smack! *(Pause.)* Okay. Where was I?

KATURIAN. Deaf boy, big long railroad tracks. *(Pause.)* Sorry.

TUPOLSKI. *(Pause.)* Okay, so, once upon a time there was this little deaf boy, couldn't hear anything, as is often the case with deaf boys. Oh yes, and it's set in China, so he was a little Chinese deaf boy. I don't know why I set it in China. Oh yes I do. I just like the look of those little Chinese kids, they're funny. *(Laughs.)* Anyway, so he's walking home from someplace one time and he's walking along these railroad tracks that stretch for miles and miles across the plains, across the Chinese plains, y'know? There's no trees, there's no nothing, there's just these fucking plains, and he's walking along these tracks and maybe he's a bit retarded too, this little kid, maybe he's a retarded little Chinese deaf kid, 'cos, I mean, he's deaf and he's walking along these fucking railroad tracks. That's fucking dangerous. What if a train comes, comes up from behind him? He ain't gonna hear it, he's gonna get squashed. So, yeah, maybe he's retarded. Okay, so there's this retarded little Chinese deaf kid walking home along these big long railroad tracks and guess what? This big fucking train starts coming up behind him.

58

But because the tracks are so long and the train is so far away, it's not gonna hit him for ages, but it *is* gonna hit him. This train is going so fast that even if the driver spotted him, there's no way he could brake in time. And this kid's really hard to see, anyway, y'know? He's like, y'know those really little, cute little Chinesey kids? They've usually got spiky-up hair? Yeah, like them. So the driver probably isn't even gonna see him. However, the kid *is* seen. You know who the kid is seen by? Well, just about a mile along the railroad tracks in the direction the little kid is heading in, there's this strange old tower, maybe a hundred feet high, and at the top of this tower there lives this strange old man, this strange old Chinese man, with one of those long Chinesey moustaches, y'know, and those squinty eyes, wa wa wa, and one of those funny little hats. And some people thought he was very wise but some people thought he was, y'know, a bit creepy, 'cos, y'know, he lives at the top of this big fucking tower. Anyway, no one had spoken to him in many many years. People didn't even know if he was alive or if he was dead. Obviously he's alive or else he wouldn't be in the story. So he's up there in his tower and he's making these mathematical computations and so forth and he's making various designs and drawings and he's doing various inventions and all that, of, like, things that haven't been invented yet, and there's a million pieces of paper all pinned up over the walls and scattered about the room and this is his whole life, all these things. The world is beneath him. These designs, these computations, are all he really cares about. And he looks out of his little arched window and he sees, just about a mile away, half a mile away now, this little deaf boy approaching, and just about two miles, maybe three miles behind him, this train thundering along. And the old man assesses the situation, quite correctly, "There is a little deaf boy walking along the railroad tracks. That little deaf boy is not going to hear the train coming up behind him. That little deaf boy is going to get squashed to bits." So ...

KATURIAN. How did he know the little boy was deaf?

TUPOLSKI. *(Pause.)* Hah?

KATURIAN. How did he know the little boy was deaf?

TUPOLSKI. *(Thinks, then.)* He saw his hearing aid. *(Katurian smiles, nods. Tupolski breathes a sigh of relief.)* Pulled that one out of the bag ... So he sees the deaf kid and he sees the train but he doesn't run down to try and save him or anything like that, like a normal person would, 'cos he's close enough if he wanted to. What does he do?

He does nothing. He does nothing but start making a little calculation on a piece of paper, just to amuse himself, a calculation based, I suppose, on the train's speed, on the length of railroad track, and on the speed the little boy's little legs are going at, a calculation to find out exactly at what point on the track this train is going to plough straight through the poor little deaf boy's little fucking back. Well, the little boy kept walking on, oblivious to all this, the train kept thundering on and on, getting closer and closer to him, and the boy was about thirty yards away from the foot of the tower when the old man finished his calculation and found that the train would smash into the boy exactly *ten yards* from the foot of the tower. *Ten yards* from the foot of the tower. And the old man ho-hummed without much interest in it all, folded his calculations into a paper aeroplane, tossed the plane out the window and got back to his work, without another thought for the poor little deaf boy. *(Pause.) Eleven yards* from the foot of the tower the little deaf boy leapt from the railroad tracks to catch the paper aeroplane. The train thundered by behind him. *(Katurian smiles.)*

KATURIAN. That's pretty good.

TUPOLSKI. "That's pretty good." That's better than all your rubbish put together. "A hundred and one ways to skewer a fucking five-year-old"?

KATURIAN. No, it's not better than all of mine, but it's pretty good.

TUPOLSKI. Excuse me, I have rescinded your permission to give me any shit, haven't I? My story is better than all of your stories.

KATURIAN. Yes, it is. And I thank you again for keeping my lesser stories safe with my file.

TUPOLSKI. Hmm.

KATURIAN. *(Pause.)* But how does that story sum up your world view anyway? Or your view of detective work, or whatever?

TUPOLSKI. Oh, don't you get it? *(Proudly.)* See, the old wise man, see, he represents *me*. He's up in his tower all day, he's doing his calculations, he hasn't got much affinity with his fellow man. The little deaf retarded boy comes along, he represents my fellow man, see? He comes along, oblivious to every fucking thing, doesn't even know there's a fucking train coming, but *I* know there's a train coming, and by the brilliance of my calculations, and by the brilliance of my throwing that paper plane at that very moment, I shall save that idiot from that train, I shall save my fellow man from those criminals, and I won't even get a word of thanks for it. That little deaf boy didn't thank the old man, did he? He just played with his fucking aeroplane. But that doesn't matter, I don't need thanks. All I need is to know that because of me toiling away with my detective work, that little boy is going to be safe from that train. *(Pause.)* Unless it's like your case, where I have to track down the train driver who's already driven straight through the poor little fucker, then reversed on all his fucking mates.

KATURIAN. *(Pause.)* So the old man *meant* for the deaf boy to catch the plane?

TUPOLSKI. Yeah.

KATURIAN. Oh.

TUPOLSKI. What, didn't you get that?

KATURIAN. No, I just thought the boy happened to catch it, like it was an accident.

TUPOLSKI. No. No, the old man wanted to save the boy. That's why he threw the plane.

KATURIAN. Ohh.

TUPOLSKI. He's really good at throwing paper planes. He's really good at everything.

KATURIAN. But then doesn't he turn away like he doesn't even care?

TUPOLSKI. No. He, like, turns away because he's so good at throwing paper planes, he doesn't even *need* to look where it's gone, on top of the fact he knows: "Ooh, little retarded boy. They love paper airplanes, don't they. He's bound to jump up and catch it." *(Pause.)* Wasn't that clear?

KATURIAN. I think it could've been more clear. *(Tupolski nods, thinking about it, then remembers his place somewhat.)* I know how you could've made it more clear ...

TUPOLSKI. Hang on! I'm not taking fucking literary advice from ya!

KATURIAN. No, I was just trying to ...

TUPOLSKI. I think *you* could've made it more clear whether the little girl you butchered three days ago was fucking alive or dead when you stuck her in the ground. I think *that* could've been made more clear. And could I make it more clear that I'm gonna get really angry in a minute and set fire to all of your stories regardless of what promises we've made? *(Tupolski picks up the stories and some matches.)* Could I make that more clear?

KATURIAN. Please, Tupolski. Your story was really good.

TUPOLSKI. My story was better than all of your stories.

KATURIAN. Your story was better than all of my stories.

TUPOLSKI. And it *was* clear that the old man wanted to save the little deaf boy.

61

KATURIAN. It was completely clear.

TUPOLSKI. *(Pause.)* You only don't like it because the little deaf boy didn't *die* at the fucking end!

KATURIAN. I *do* like it, Tupolski. And this isn't anything to do with anything. About burning my stories or anything. I really liked your story. I'd've been proud to have written it. I would.

TUPOLSKI. *(Pause.)* Yeah?

KATURIAN. Yeah. *(Pause. Tupolski puts the stories down.)*

TUPOLSKI. I wasn't going to burn them anyway. I'm a man of my word. If a person keeps his word, I keep my word.

KATURIAN. I know that. I respect that. And I know you don't care if I respect that or not, but either way, I respect that.

TUPOLSKI. Well, I respect that you respect that. Ah, aren't we all cosy? It's almost a shame I have to shoot you in the head in twenty minutes. *(Tupolski smiles. Katurian thinks about his death for the first time in a while.)*

KATURIAN. Mm. *(Tupolski stops smiling. Pause.)*

TUPOLSKI. No, I ... Some of your stories are very good too. I did like some of them.

KATURIAN. Which ones?

TUPOLSKI. *(Pause.)* There was something about "The Pillowman" that stayed with me. There was something gentle about it. *(Pause.)* And the idea of, if a child died, alone, through some accident, he wasn't really alone. He had this kind, soft person with him, to hold his hand and whatnot. And that it was the child's choice, somehow. Made it somewhat, reassuring, somehow. That it wasn't just a stupid waste.

KATURIAN. *(Nods. Pause.)* Did you lose a child?

TUPOLSKI. *(Pause.)* Unlike old Ariel, I don't go into those sorts of things with the condemned. *(Katurian nods. Sad pause.)* Son drowned. *(Pause.)* Fishing on his own. *(Pause.)* Silly. *(Katurian nods. Tupolski puts the battery back into the cabinet.)*

KATURIAN. What happens from here on in?

TUPOLSKI. We get the word back about the mute girl ... *(Tupolski takes a black hood out of the cabinet, shows it daintily to Katurian, back and front.)* ... we put this hood over your head, we take you to the room next door, we shoot you through the head. *(Pause.)* Is that right? No. We take you to the room next door, *then* we put the hood on you, *then* we shoot you through the head. If we put the hood on you *before* we take you to the room next door, y'know, you might bump into something, hurt yourself.

KATURIAN. Why the room next door? Why not here?

TUPOLSKI. The room next door, it's easier to mop up.

KATURIAN. *(Pause.)* Do you do it out of the blue, like, just out of the blue, or do you give me a minute to say a prayer or something?

TUPOLSKI. Well, first I sing a song about a little pony and then Ariel takes out his hedgehog. Y'know, his execution hedgehog? And when the hedgehog's out, well, you've got either thirteen or twenty-seven seconds left, depending on the size of the hedgehog. *(Pause.)* If I'm gonna do it out of the blue, I'm not gonna *tell you* I'm gonna do it out of the blue, am I?! Jesus! For a supposed genius writer-stroke-psycho-killer, you're a bit fucking thick! *(Pause.)* From when the hood goes on you've got about ten seconds. So, y'know, keep the Latin chants to a minimum.

KATURIAN. Thank you.

TUPOLSKI. You're welcome. *(Tupolski tosses the hood on the table in front of Katurian. Pause.)*

KATURIAN. No, I just want to think a few thoughts for my brother.

TUPOLSKI. Uh-huh? For your brother, yeah? Not for the three little kids you murdered, but for your brother.

KATURIAN. That's right. Not for the three little kids that I murdered, but for my brother. *(Door opens, Ariel enters, dumbstruck, blank-faced. He slowly moves towards Katurian.)*

TUPOLSKI. Have they found her? *(Ariel reaches Katurian, who is getting scared. Ariel places a hand on Katurian's head and, clutching his hair, tilts Katurian's head back, gently, staring down at him.)*

ARIEL. *(Quietly.)* What the hell is the matter with you? Exactly what the hell is the matter with you? *(Katurian can't answer. Ariel gently releases him and slowly goes back to the door.)*

TUPOLSKI. Ariel?

ARIEL. Mm?

TUPOLSKI. Have they found her?

ARIEL. Yes, they found her.

TUPOLSKI. And she was dead, right? *(Ariel is at the door.)*

ARIEL. No. *(Katurian puts his head in his hands in horror.)*

TUPOLSKI. She was still alive? *(Ariel beckons to someone at the door-way. A mute girl of about eight, her face, hair, clothes, shoes painted totally bright green, enters, smiling happily. She says hello to the two men in sign language.)*

ARIEL. They found her down there by the wishing well, in a little Wendy house there. She had three little piglets with her. She had

63

plenty of food and water. So did the piglets, in fact. She seems quite happy about it all, don't you, Maria? *(Ariel signs, "Are you happy?" to her. Smiling, she signs back at some length.)* She says yes, she *is* quite happy but can she keep the piglets? *(Pause.)* I said I'd ask you. *(Tupolski just stares at them both, stunned. Pause.)* I said I'd ask *you* about the piglets.

TUPOLSKI. What? Oh. Yes, she can keep the piglets. *(Ariel gives her the thumbs-up. She starts leaping about, squealing in delight. Katurian smiles slightly.)*

ARIEL. Yes, yes, but let's get you cleaned up first and get you to your mummy and daddy. They've been worried about you. *(Ariel takes her hand, she waves goodbye to everyone happily, and he leads her out of the door. Tupolski and Katurian's faces slowly turn from the door and to each other. After a second, Ariel slowly re-enters, closing the door behind him.)* They found a big pot of green paint down there with her, you know that kind of glow-in-the-dark paint they have in railway tunnels? So, plenty of prints if we need them. And they found the skeletons of the parents just where he said, by the wishing well. So. He confesses to the murder of two people we knew nothing about, and he confesses to the murder of a girl who wasn't actually murdered.

TUPOLSKI. Why?

ARIEL. Why? You're asking me why?

TUPOLSKI. Yes, I am.

ARIEL. Uh-huh? Well, Tupolski, you know what? *You're* the Number One, *you* fucking figure it out.

TUPOLSKI. I'll have no more insubordination from you today, Ariel.

ARIEL. Er, yes, you will.

TUPOLSKI. In which case, you're on report to the Commandant as of now.

ARIEL. You don't seem very happy that the little girl's still alive! Even *this* bloke seems happy that the little girl's still alive! You just seem upset he's fucked up your paperwork! *(Tupolski fishes through the stories to find a particular one.)*

TUPOLSKI. Obviously the girl was painted green and put with the piglets in order to act out …

ARIEL. To act out "The Little Green Pig" story. Brilliant, Tupolski. You must've got that from the green paint and the piglets. The question is, why? Why didn't they kill her too? And why did he say he did?

TUPOLSKI. Shh, I'm reading through the story, and see if there are any clues.

ARIEL. *(Laughs.)* We could just ask him!

TUPOLSKI. I'm reading through this, I said!

ARIEL. *(To Katurian.)* Can *you* fill us in on why the mute girl's still alive?

KATURIAN. *(Pause.)* No. No, I can't. But I'm glad she is, though. I'm glad she is.

ARIEL. I *believe* you're glad she is. I *believe* you're glad she is. I believe you're gladder she is than *he* fucking is. I will ask you another question, based on a little hunch I've just got, 'cos *I'm* getting hunches now, too. I think Mr. Tupolski's fucking *detective prowess* is rubbing off on me. The little Jewish boy whose toes you cut off and let bleed to death. What colour was his hair?

KATURIAN. What?

ARIEL. What colour was his hair?

KATURIAN. Browny-black. It was a browny-black sort of colour.

ARIEL. "It was a browny-black sort of colour." Pretty good. Considering he was a little Jew boy, "It was a browny-black sort of colour." Pretty good. It's a shame his mum was fucking Irish, and her son closely resembled a red fucking setter. Do you want some questions about the girl on the heath?

KATURIAN. No.

ARIEL. No. Because you didn't kill either of those two children, did you?

KATURIAN. No.

ARIEL. You never even saw those two children, did you?

KATURIAN. No.

ARIEL. Did you tell your brother to kill them?

KATURIAN. I never knew anything about any of this until today.

ARIEL. Did your brother kill your parents, also?

KATURIAN. *I* killed my parents.

ARIEL. The only killing we can definitely pin on you is the killing of your brother. In light of the extenuating circumstances, I doubt it highly that you would be executed for it. I would therefore think very carefully before admitting to the killing of …

KATURIAN. *I* killed my parents. *(Pause.)* *I* killed my parents.

ARIEL. I believe you did. *(Pause.)* But you didn't kill any children, did you? *(Katurian shakes his lowered head.)* Your witness, Tupolski. *(Ariel lights a cigarette. Tupolski, having regained his composure somewhat, sits back down.)*

TUPOLSKI. Very good work, Ariel.

ARIEL. Thank you, Tupolski.

TUPOLSKI. And, by the way, I *was* happy that the little girl was still alive. I was just trying not to let my true emotions come out at work, that's all.

ARIEL. Oh, I see …

TUPOLSKI. You see? *(Pause.)* Hmm. So, um, just out of my own personal curiosity, just before we execute you for these three other murders, why did you confess to killing the children, Mr. Katurian?

KATURIAN. You had me for killing Michal. As soon as you found the third child you'd have me for killing my parents. I thought that if I tied myself into all of it, like you wanted me to, at least I'd be able to save my stories. At least I'd have that. *(Pause.)* At least I'd have that.

TUPOLSKI. Hmm. That's a shame then, isn't it?

KATURIAN. What's a shame?

TUPOLSKI. Our saving your stories was based on you confessing truthfully as regards the whole of this sorry business. Evidently from what you're saying now about not having killed the other two children and evidently from all the green fucking paint that's been traipsed all over my fucking floor, your confession wasn't completely truthful, was it? And so, obviously, if your confession wasn't completely truthful, your stories fucking burn. *(Tupolski gets the bin, pours lighter fuel in, gets matches.)*

KATURIAN. You're not being serious.

TUPOLSKI. There's your hood. Put it on, please. I'm trying to get a fire started.

KATURIAN. Ariel, please…?

TUPOLSKI. Ariel? Is it true that, as honourable men, we promised not to burn his stories if he made a truthful confession?

ARIEL. Ah Jesus, Tupolski …

TUPOLSKI. Is it true, yes or no, that we promised not to burn his stories if he made a truthful confession?

ARIEL. Yes. It's true.

TUPOLSKI. And did he confess to killing a Jew boy he didn't kill?

ARIEL. Yes, he did.

TUPOLSKI. And did he confess to killing a girl with razor blades he also didn't kill?

ARIEL. Yes, he did.

TUPOLSKI. And did he confess to killing that irritating green kid who isn't even fucking dead?

ARIEL. Yes, he did confess to it.

TUPOLSKI. Are we not, then, within our rights, as honourable men, to burn all of Mr. Katurian's work?

KATURIAN. Ariel …

ARIEL. *(Sadly.)* We *are* within our rights.

TUPOLSKI. We *are* within our rights. So, we've got about four hundred stories here, and if we round up those few copies of *The Libertad* he had a story in, that'll be his whole life's work, right? That'll be his whole life's work. *(Tupolski weighs the stories in his hands.)* Doesn't add up to much. Should I put some lighter fuel on his stories too, or is that a bit dangerous? I'm worried I might singe myself.

KATURIAN. Ariel, please …

TUPOLSKI. Put the hood on, I said. *(Tupolski lights the fire in the bin, still holding the stories.)*

KATURIAN. Ariel!

TUPOLSKI. *(Pause.)* Ariel?

ARIEL. *(Pause.)* I know all this isn't your fault. I know you didn't kill the children. I know you didn't want to kill your brother, and I know you killed your parents for all the right reasons, and I'm sorry for you, I'm really sorry for you, and I've never said that to anybody in custody before. But at the end of the day, I never liked your stories in the first fucking place. Y'know? *(Ariel takes the stories from Tupolski.)* You'd better put the hood on. *(Katurian goes to put the hood on, then stops.)*

KATURIAN. I thought you were supposed to take me next door first and I put it on in there?

TUPOLSKI. No, no, we shoot you in here. I was just mucking around. Just kneel down over there somewhere, so you don't splash me.

KATURIAN. But will you give me ten seconds from when the hood goes on, or were you mucking around then too?

TUPOLSKI. Errm …

ARIEL. We'll give you ten seconds …

TUPOLSKI. We'll give you ten seconds, I'm kidding, I'm kidding. *(Katurian kneels on the floor. Tupolski takes out his gun and cocks it. Katurian stares sadly at Ariel.)*

KATURIAN. I was a good writer. *(Pause.)* It was all I ever wanted to be. *(Pause.)* And I was. And I was.

TUPOLSKI. "Was" being the operative word.

KATURIAN. *(Pause.)* Yes. "Was" being the operative word. *(Katurian pulls the hood on. Tupolski takes aim.)*

TUPOLSKI. Ten. Nine. Eight. Seven. Six. Five. Four … *(Tupolski shoots Katurian in the head. He drops to the floor, dead, blood slowly*

seeping from the hood.)
ARIEL. Oh what did you do that for?
TUPOLSKI. What did I do what for?
ARIEL. You said you'd give him ten. That wasn't very nice.
TUPOLSKI. Ariel, what exactly *is* nice about shooting a man on his knees with a bag on his head?
ARIEL. Even so.
TUPOLSKI. Listen, I've had enough whingeing out of you for one day. What's the matter with you? We've cleared up the case, haven't we, whichever way you look at it? Well, haven't we?
ARIEL. I suppose.
TUPOLSKI. That's all the more sweets for you when you're seventy, isn't it? *(Ariel sighs.)* Listen, get the paperwork finished, get this room cleaned up and get those stories burned. Okay? I'd better speak to that mute kid's parents, warn them about the piglets. *(Tupolski exits. Ariel adds a little more lighter fuel to the fire, then looks at the sheaf of stories in his hands. The dead Katurian slowly gets to his feet, takes the hood off to reveal his bloody, bullet-shattered head, observes Ariel at the table, and speaks.)*
KATURIAN. In the seven and three-quarter seconds he was given before he died, Katurian Katurian tried to think up a final story in lieu of a prayer for his brother. What he came up with was more of a footnote to a story, and the footnote was this ... *(Michal is revealed leaning in the doorway in low light.)* A happy, healthy little boy named Michal Katurian, on the eve of the night that his parents were to start torturing him for seven consecutive years, was visited by a man made of all fluffy pillows and a big smiley mouth, and the man sat with Michal and talked to him a while and told him about the horrific life he was to lead and where it was to end for him, with his only, beloved brother smothering his life out on a cold prison floor, and the man suggested to Michal that wouldn't it be better if he did away with himself there and then and avoided all that horror? And Michal said ...
MICHAL. But if I do away with myself, my brother will never get to hear me being tortured, will he?
KATURIAN. "No," said the Pillowman.
MICHAL. But if my brother never gets to hear me being tortured, he may never write the stories he's going to write, might he?
KATURIAN. "That's true," said the Pillowman. And Michal thought about it a while and said ...
MICHAL. Well, I think we should probably just keep things the

way they are, then, with me being tortured and him hearing and all of that business, 'cos I think I'm going to really like my brother's stories. I think I'm going to really like them. *(Lights fade on Michal.)*

KATURIAN. The story was going to finish in fashionably down-beat mode, with Michal going through all that torment, with Katurian writing all those stories, only to have them burned from the world by a bulldog of a policeman. The story *was* going to finish that way, but was of course cut short by a bullet blowing his brains out two seconds too soon. And maybe it was best that the story didn't finish that way, as it wouldn't have been quite accurate. Because, for reasons known only to himself, the bulldog of a policeman chose not to put the stories in the burning trash, but placed them carefully with Katurian's case file, which he then sealed away to remain unopened for fifty-odd years. *(Ariel puts the stories in the box file.)* A fact which would have ruined the writer's fashionably downbeat ending, but was somehow … somehow … more in keeping with the spirit of the thing. *(Ariel snuffs out the fire in the bin with water, as the lights, very slowly, fade to black.)*

End of Play

PROPERTY LIST

Cigarettes
Lighter/matches
Toys
Paints
Pens
Paper
Note in red writing
Box file containing papers (TUPOLSKI)
Blindfold (KATURIAN)
Metal box containing five bloody toes (TUPOLSKI)
Bloodied white cloth (ARIEL)
Axe (KATURIAN)
Drills (MOTHER, FATHER)
Pillow (KATURIAN, MICHAL)
False beard (GIRL)
Sandals (GIRL)
Dust (GIRL)
Cross (MOTHER, FATHER)
Shovel (MOTHER, FATHER)
Dirt (MOTHER, FATHER)
Gun (TUPOLSKI)
Hand-drawn map (TUPOLSKI)
Large battery with electrodes attached (ARIEL)
Black hood (TUPOLSKI)
Lighter fuel (TUPOLSKI)
Stage blood (KATURIAN)
Water (ARIEL)

SOUND EFFECTS

Noises of torture (drilling sounds, screams)

NEW PLAYS

★ **CLYBOURNE PARK by Bruce Norris.** WINNER OF THE 2011 PULITZER PRIZE AND 2012 TONY AWARD. Act One takes place in 1959 as community leaders try to stop the sale of a home to a black family. Act Two is set in the same house in the present day as the now predominantly African-American neighborhood battles to hold its ground. "Vital, sharp-witted and ferociously smart." *—NY Times.* "A theatrical treasure...Indisputably, uproariously funny." *—Entertainment Weekly.* [4M, 3W] ISBN: 978-0-8222-2697-0

★ **WATER BY THE SPOONFUL by Quiara Alegría Hudes.** WINNER OF THE 2012 PULITZER PRIZE. A Puerto Rican veteran is surrounded by the North Philadelphia demons he tried to escape in the service. "This is a very funny, warm, and yes uplifting play." *—Hartford Courant.* "The play is a combination poem, prayer and app on how to cope in an age of uncertainty, speed and chaos." *—Variety.* [4M, 3W] ISBN: 978-0-8222-2716-8

★ **RED by John Logan.** WINNER OF THE 2010 TONY AWARD. Mark Rothko has just landed the biggest commission in the history of modern art. But when his young assistant, Ken, gains the confidence to challenge him, Rothko faces the agonizing possibility that his crowning achievement could also become his undoing. "Intense and exciting." *—NY Times.* "Smart, eloquent entertainment." *—New Yorker.* [2M] ISBN: 978-0-8222-2483-9

★ **VENUS IN FUR by David Ives.** Thomas, a beleaguered playwright/director, is desperate to find an actress to play Vanda, the female lead in his adaptation of the classic sadomasochistic tale *Venus in Fur.* "Ninety minutes of good, kinky fun." *—NY Times.* "A fast-paced journey into one man's entrapment by a clever, vengeful female." *—Associated Press.* [1M, 1W] ISBN: 978-0-8222-2603-1

★ **OTHER DESERT CITIES by Jon Robin Baitz.** Brooke returns home to Palm Springs after a six-year absence and announces that she is about to publish a memoir dredging up a pivotal and tragic event in the family's history—a wound they don't want reopened. "Leaves you feeling both moved and gratifyingly sated." *—NY Times.* "A genuine pleasure." *—NY Post.* [2M, 3W] ISBN: 978-0-8222-2605-5

★ **TRIBES by Nina Raine.** Billy was born deaf into a hearing family and adapts brilliantly to his family's unconventional ways, but it's not until he meets Sylvia, a young woman on the brink of deafness, that he finally understands what it means to be understood. "A smart, lively play." *—NY Times.* "[A] bright and boldly provocative drama." *—Associated Press.* [3M, 2W] ISBN: 978-0-8222-2751-9

DRAMATISTS PLAY SERVICE, INC.
440 Park Avenue South, New York, NY 10016 212-683-8960 Fax 212-213-1539
postmaster@dramatists.com   www.dramatists.com